The Invisible Organization

The Invisible Organization

How Informal Networks Can Lead Organizational Change

NEIL FARMER

Routledge
Taylor & Francis Group

LONDON AND NEW YORK

First published in paperback 2024

First published 2008 by Gower Publishing

Published 2016 by Routledge
4 Park Square, Milton Park, Abingdon, Oxon OX14 4RN

and by Routledge
605 Third Avenue, New York, NY 10158

Routledge is an imprint of the Taylor & Francis Group, an informa business

British Library Cataloguing in Publication Data
Farmer, Neil
  The invisible organization : how informal networks can lead
  organizational change
  1. Organizational change 2. Business networks
  I. Title
  658.4'06

Library of Congress Cataloging-in-Publication Data
Farmer, Neil.
  The invisible organization : how informal networks can lead organizational change / by Neil Farmer.
    p. cm.
  Includes bibliographical references and index.
  ISBN 978-0-566-08877-3
  1. Organizational change. 2. Industrial management--Social aspects. I. Title.

HD58.8.F367 2008
658.4'06--dc22
                                                          2008019119

ISBN 13: 978-0-566-08877-3 (hbk)
ISBN 13: 978-1-03-283872-4 (pbk)
ISBN 13: 978-1-315-23888-3 (ebk)

DOI: 10.4324/9781315238883

Contents

List of Figures

About the Author

Neil Farmer is a leading, innovative business change consultant.

Neil started his consultancy career in 1981 when he joined the ground-breaking IT research and consultancy firm Butler Cox. His early experience included extensive research on the business impact of IT, a wide variety of IT and business strategies, and advising on very large IT implementation projects. In the 1990s, his interests moved on to business transformation, when he increasingly worked on major business process re-engineering programmes.

From 1988 to 1996, he founded and headed one of the UK's top change research groups – the Farringdon Forum Club, while still spending almost half his time working with consultancy clients. During this period, he carried out extensive research into business change, becoming increasingly focused on a single profound question – *why does so much business change fail*?

This work culminated in the controversial book 'Total Business Design' published by John Wiley & Sons in 1996. As well as being highly critical of management 'fads and fashions', the book highlighted for the first time the importance of local influencers and informal networks in successful business change.

Over the last 10 years, Neil has become that rare breed of consultant – an individual who cannot be classified as a specific consultancy commodity. Despite this, he has found his niche – the consultant you rely on when business change becomes challenging. His clients include large Business Process Outsourcing suppliers (Siemens Business Services, BT and Xchanging) as well as household names such as Nationwide Building Society, National Savings, Liverpool City Council, Lloyds of London and Friends Provident. His latest challenge – still a 'work in progress' and hopefully not 'a bridge too far' is transforming the public sectors in several African countries – Tanzania, Libya and Botswana.

'The Invisible Organization' highlights the main lessons and practical techniques learnt and developed by Neil and his colleagues on the path to consistently successful business change.

Neil has a BSc honours degree in Chemistry from Sussex University and an MBA from Warwick Business School.

Reviews for *The Invisible Organization*

'If only we had this book when HR set out on our journey to gain professional recognition and make a strategic contribution. Its a little way out, it takes chances, it makes us vulnerable and it finally helps HR stand up and be counted. An exciting and refreshing rethink on HR's contribution to organizational change.'

Graham White, Director of HR,
Westminster City Council

'I like this book, it is both appropriately theoretical and easy to understand, offering tangible approaches that can relatively easily be adopted. I have long believed in the power of informal networks. Whilst senior managers are crucial to the success of change programmes, their commitment alone will not secure a desired result ... we take action when we see those close to us who are trusted lead the way.

In The Invisible Organization Neil Farmer shows deep understanding of how organizations REALLY work.'

Liane Hornsey, European HR Director,
Google

'Many companies are attempting to change the way they operate; however many initiatives are doomed to fail before the first presentation is given. Grand ideas will remain simply ideas without the mobilisation and activation of the workforce. This book highlights the hidden resources which every company has and how to engage them – but more than that, it draws attention to the real influencers and the role they play.'

Dr Colin Herron, Manager: Manufacturing and Productivity,
One NorthEast

'I totally agree with the concept of Organizational Network Analysis described in this book. At MWH we have been using ONAs around the organization for some time and find them very relevant to forming a well functioning organization. It provides a real insight into how to leverage change in an organization because it is so much easier to spot the real change agents. In addition to using them in house we have also used them with some of our clients to determine how to accelerate change and to identify critical knowledge within their organization.'

Ken Farrer, Vice Chairman,
MWH UK

'Coping with continuous change is one of the biggest challenges facing management in today's world. Neil Farmer's book gives some interesting new insights into how this can be achieved.'

Sir George Cox

'The Invisible Organization *highlights the paradigms shift taking place in companies globally. This book does an excellent job of outlining the change in communications patterns of our employees and the power informal networks have on productivity and innovation.'*

Dona E. Roche-Tarry , Managing Partner, Board Services,
CTPartners (UK) Ltd

'Making real change happen in the workplace is not achieved by senior management deciding everything and then telling everyone else what will happen. Real change comes from working as a team throughout the whole structure, valuing the opinions of everyone and using staff at all levels to influence each other and make change happen. Embrace the ingenuity of your whole workforce instead of relying on a small group who are regularly too far away from the reality of what really happens anyway!'

Mark Linley, Manufacturing Director,
Hallmark Cards PLC

'Much has been said about leaders who lead the business forward and managers who push it from behind. In the real business world, however, most of the natural leaders are hidden within the ranks. By engaging influencers working through informal networks, you release a whole new generation of naturally effective leaders from top to bottom in your organization.* The Invisible Organization *shows how to deliver exceptional value for both the organization and the influencers themselves.'*

David White, Managing Director,
Tanley Ltd (leading advisers on outsourcing)

'I really enjoyed Neil Farmer's new book. It is engaging and insightful, managing that difficult balance between a sound theoretical base and practical clarity. The writing style is very interesting and kept my attention throughout. It offers real help to professionals managing business transformation from the first chapter, both exposing fallacies and highlighting the value – and traps – of ONA. It makes a cogent argument for what is going wrong beneath the surface of organizations and how this invisible force can be harnessed. I am looking forward to putting some of these ideas into practice.'

Kevin Parry,[*] Founder,
Cogenic

---

[*]   Kevin Parry is an acknowledged industry expert in programme management, transformation design and change. Before setting up Cogenic, he was a Programme Director and Change Leader in BT plc, working on many major change programmes.

Acknowledgements

This book is dedicated to all those senior executives, would-be change agents, and consultants who have not only had the courage to admit to levels of failure, but are also prepared to discuss them, learn the lessons and move on to more successful approaches.

The author's gratitude is extended to the client organizations that have enabled new techniques to be tried, tested and developed during major change programmes over recent years. Also to friends and associates in the consulting community who lent their experience, advice and encouragement. In particular Stuart Wilde for his help with the many projects at Siemens Business Services, Neil Grogan for his introductions and encouragement at BT, David White for his introductions and practical support at Xchanging and Andrew Loach for his guidance on building client interest in the practical use of informal networks.

Worthy of special mention are:

Art Benjamin, one of Canada's 'all time' top consultants who in 1997 gave the author the following words of advice:

> 'If you really want to address the root causes of business change failure, look hard at the people side of change. The techniques used in HR and change management today are still in the dark ages. If you want to make a real difference, take a deep breath and go for it!'

Denis Bourne, a very successful HR consultant and leading-edge software developer who has the temerity to believe that senior managers should use approaches that work, rather than those that happen to be fashionable. His 'Magus Toolbox' products are used throughout this book to create informal network diagrams. Denis has networked a group of innovative consultants across Europe (including the author) to build awareness and consulting capability in the practical use of informal networks. His encouragement in times of stress (usually when yet another potential client – typically a command and control-type CEO – is not returning phone calls) has been invaluable. He made a major contribution to the 'Reflections' section of this book.

Sir George Cox, the author's former boss who went on to become Director General of the Institute of Directors. Not only did George edit the author's first book (*Total Business Design*) but he has given much needed encouragement over the years as recognition for the business value of influencers and informal networks grew very slowly. Allegedly he also coined the prophetic phrase:

> *'Just because you are right does not mean that you are going to be rich!'*

Thanks to you all.

Preface

The birth of an insight

The ability to initiate and carry out change has become a key determinant of success in today's world. The business that cannot deal with change won't simply be unsuccessful, it will not survive.

The problem is that most organizations still find change difficult to carry out – routinely, confidently, to time and on budget, with the desired results and without causing widespread disruption. This book takes a new perspective on the issue.

In all businesses there are two organizations: one that is shown on the formal organization chart and another that exists in reality. The latter is made up not of job titles or formal lines of authority but rather of 'influencers' and other individuals within a variety of social networks. These informal networks have an impact on how employees think and behave. They can be both positive and negative, but to attempt to drive change through without recognizing them is courting disaster.

Only in the last 5 years have influencers and informal networks been used effectively to determine how people are selected, organized and motivated. Influencer mapping across all levels of an organization can now be laid over key points in personal network maps to illustrate clearly the hidden realities (see Figure P1.1 overleaf). These developments are enabling businesses to transform the 'weakest link' in modern business design – the people element.

We can now see the full impact of this new capability. Business change will much more often deliver the desired benefits the first time round without people-impacted delays and cost overruns; knowledge management and inter-organizational collaboration will come of age; the tired old HR models for managing employees will be radically refreshed; and the future of white collar outsourcing will be viewed very differently.

Put simply, we are beginning to experience a major practical breakthrough in the people element of organizational design. The benefits are available today, if you can discard much of the management 'command and control' baggage, and if you know where to look.

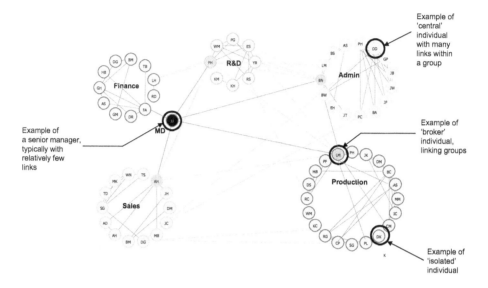

Note: This type of informal network diagram can be produced by a wide variety of organizational 'scans', ranging from the identification of key influencers, through communication, knowledge and data sources and value-added patterns, to problem identification and analysis. Changes in specific analysis patterns over time can indicate the success or otherwise of interventions/remedial actions.

Software used: Magus Networker

Figure P1.1 Typical patterns within informal networks

'The Invisible Organization': Highlights of the Book

Unlike the formal leadership structure of a traditional organization chart, in reality there is not a single or small group of leaders in organizations but lots of them. Some leaders influence the views of many people and some of just one or two, influencing and 'leading' at all levels across your organization. The CEO, senior management team and all of the formal management hierarchy put together can probably identify less than a third of these dispersed 'leaders' and the management team's combined power to influence represents less than 20 per cent of the total potential influencing capability across all employees. More than three quarters of the leaders in your organization are probably not in the management hierarchy at all!

This is 'The Invisible Organization': a world of influencers and informal employee networks that most accurately reflects the 'real world' in your business.

The fundamental idea behind this book is that business can best be managed through a balanced implementation of formal and informal networks. The formal networks are represented by organization charts, business processes, systems and formal procedures. The informal networks are made up of an array of ingredients: influence networks, communication networks, knowledge networks; even sub-networks of individuals experiencing bad behaviours, process problems or missed opportunities. All your previous business designs have been based on management control through formal networks alone. For the first time, CEOs and senior managers can now seek to design and build their organizations by using the most effective mix of both the formal and informal elements – by getting the balance right.

Until the late 1990s, the practical use of informal networks was inhibited by difficulties in accuracy and reliability in two main areas:

1.　Identifying the key influencers at all levels across an organization: those who are both highly influential and by nature change-positive, or at least open-minded on change.

2.　Identifying informal networks where sensitive information is required, particularly where named individuals are failing to perform effectively.

The breakthrough came when iterative interviews were used to identify accurately relevant key influencers at all levels. (This process begins by interviewing known change champions, getting their views on change-positive and open-minded influencers and then progressively repeating the interview process across the organization – with only the individuals mentioned being interviewed at each successive stage, until no new names emerge. This eliminates major distortions inherent in representative sampling due to the inputs of change-negative and disinterested individuals.) Once the key influencers at all levels are known, they are then selectively engaged to guide the questionnaire design, sample selection and results analysis process that results in much more accurate and relevant informal networks being uncovered.

Now that these two difficulties have been overcome, extensive experience over the last 5 to 10 years shows that balanced formal and informal networks can be used to resolve effectively many of the intractable problems that have beset businesses in the past. Successful examples range from business turnarounds, large international mergers and acquisitions, major process and system-driven change programmes, fundamental cultural change and continuous improvement, through to organizational problem solving, succession planning and employee motivation on a day-to-day basis. It is an approach that offers a permanent alternative to the stubborn 70 per cent failure rule for business change initiatives.

It is in the management areas, however, that the main impacts of the effective use of balanced networks will be experienced (see Chapter 5: Throwing out those tired old HR models). The high-performance workplace of the future will incorporate the following very different roles:

- Executive leadership – to develop strategic direction, with a little autocracy and a lot of collaboration for effective change implementation.

- Middle managers – to act as coordinators and enablers for the 'high-performance workplace', guiding and integrating a plethora of ideas and initiatives, mainly from below, all within the context of an agreed business strategy.

- First-line management – the *real* people managers in the 'high-performance workplace' – most will be key influencers, so some 60 per cent of incumbents probably need to be replaced – often with more women than men.

- HR Managers – with a key role, to inform and guide senior managers in optimizing the people resource through formal and informal mechanisms – but most won't make the transition.

- Local influencers and those with extensive personal networks – get much bigger roles across all forms of business change – as these key individuals become the *real* change agents.

Balanced networks will also have a profound impact on outsourcing decisions. In many cases, outsource suppliers are forced to overcome one fundamental hurdle that does not apply if change is implemented internally – they have to fragment at least some of the relevant informal personal networks! Because of the fundamental importance of using informal networks to drive successful business change, these increased pressures on outsource suppliers may well shape the future direction of the white collar outsourcing industry. The traditional outsourcing model will be replaced progressively by an in-house 'transform-operate-transfer' model. This model is based on the service provider delivering a core team of change design and implementation specialists who will take transitional responsibility for selected areas of the business and will deliver agreed target changes in agreed timescales.

Once you know who the key players are across informal networks, it becomes possible to implement practical, effective 'deep' leadership – the fruitless search to develop 'super managers' is replaced by practical leadership through 'super networks'. The real super managers are then those who can best engage and focus key individuals across the leadership 'super network'.

VIEWS AND CLUES

Throughout this book, we draw the reader's attention to selected extracts from newspapers, magazines and published reports.

These selections of 'Views and Clues' contain clues as to the major trends and underlying drivers that determine why business change fails and how future change can be successfully implemented. They also set the scene for fundamental changes in the ways that employees are managed, engaged and motivated.

One reason why big organizations become inefficient is communication failure. Subordinates have lots of reasons not to tell bosses the truth. They don't want to burden 'busy' people with detail, or rock the boat, or be victim of 'shoot the messenger' syndrome. The upshot of this was famously described by the late Kenneth Boulding: 'The larger and more authoritarian the organization, the better the chance that its top decision-makers will be operating in purely imaginary worlds'

Source: *We put up with terrible, inept government. Why?, The Times,* 30 May 2007

In Britain, there is a growing anxiety about the standard of business leadership and decision making. Accenture, the global consulting, technology and outsourcing company, carries out a review, The High Performance Workforce Study, every 18 months or so. It regularly finds that leadership is one of the top three concerns reported by senior executives.

Source: *Farming out isn't always the answer, The Sunday Times,* 10 June 2007

The Failure of Business Leadership

Over the last three decades, the rule of thumb figure for successful change programmes that involve fundamentally changing the way that people work has stubbornly averaged about 30 per cent. In other words, about 70 per cent of change programmes fail to meet most (or any) of the original business objectives. This basic failure is often compounded by time and cost overruns, some of which are so large as to swamp the initial, often naïve or politically-wishful, estimates.

The yawning gap between strategy and implementation

The change programme failure rates shown in Figure 1.1 have been used by the author as key slides in senior management presentations for over a decade. Over that long period, the latest research updates have oscillated up and down but

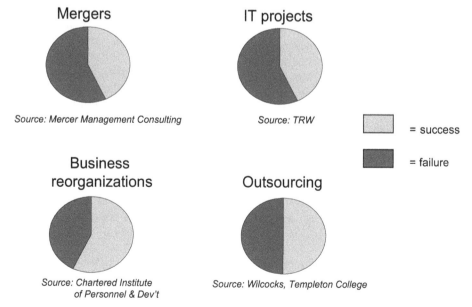

Figure 1.1   High failure rates in organizational change

the underlying trend has been constant. Putting it bluntly, there is something very wrong with the way that almost all senior executives (and their internal – or contracted external – programme managers) are dealing with profound business change.

Although technical problems are sometimes the root cause of failures in major organizational change, they tend to be symptomatic of the wider problems associated with the programme and are rarely the sole or main cause. The biggest single cause of business change failure by far is 'people problems'.

VIEWS AND CLUES

If, as one (hospital) consultant put it, gaining these benefits for the NHS is 'about putting together the broken processes', why is government policy so intent on fragmenting them? Isn't separating out activities and hiving them off to the private sector (what the Keep Our NHS Public campaign, www.keepournhspublic.com, calls 'patchwork privatisation') the very antithesis of Toyota-like flow? Yep, that's exactly what it is. Since the government is obsessed with traditional economies of scale, most private-sector providers are engaged to optimize activities (building hospitals, offshoring medical secretaries) rather than to create economies of flow. Worse, under the profit motive, they have no incentive to streamline the activity or, God forbid, get rid of it altogether, as Toyota would.

Source: *In the drive to save the NHS, I'm choosing a Toyota, The Observer,* 14 January 2007

Private equity funds last year went on an unprecedented $725bn (£367bn) global buying spree – *a figure outstripping the entire economy of the Netherlands. Figures out next week estimate that buyout funds, which have cut a swathe through global businesses and now employ over a fifth of employees in Britain's private sector, can draw on a war chest of $2 trillion to fund acquisitions – enough to buy McDonald's 38 times.*

Source: *No firm is safe from private equity, The Observer,* 20 May 2007

The leaders of 130 000 police officers have drawn up a dossier of 'lunacy' on Britain's streets. They say that children are being arrested for throwing cream buns and bits of cucumber while adults are getting criminal records for offences that merit nothing more than a ticking-off. The pressure to get results (to meet targets) is so bad, they say, that officers are criminalising and alienating their traditional supporters in Middle England and many are so disillusioned that they are considering quitting.

Source: *We are making ludicrous arrests just to meet our targets, The Times,* 15 May 2007

IT project failures have been the subject of analysis over recent decades and research has shown that direct or indirect 'people problems' are the dominant cause of IT project failure. A 2004 CHAOS survey by The Standish Group, outlined below, is reasonably typical. The survey analyzed the top three reasons for success and failure across three IT project outcomes – successful projects, 'challenged projects' (where the end result was achieved but problems were experienced, such as time or cost overruns) and failed projects.

Top three reasons for IT project success/failure from the CHAOS survey were:

- *Successful projects*
    1. User involvement
    2. Executive management support
    3. Clear statement of requirements
- *Challenged projects (cost/timescale overruns, and so on)*
    1. Lack of user input
    2. Incomplete requirements and specifications
    3. Changing requirements and specifications
- *Failed projects*
    1. Incomplete requirements
    2. Lack of user involvement
    3. Lack of resources

Research into the underlying causes of failure in other types of major business change initiatives (such as mergers, transformations, outsourcing, and so on) also highlight the dominance of 'people problems'.

Managers are not good at implementing business change

Despite professional adherence to change methods and a proliferation of increasingly sophisticated technology and process design tools, the success rates for ambitious business change programmes that impact on how people work day-to-day remains depressingly low. One of the most recent surveys, conducted online by McKinsey Quarterly in 2006, showed only 38 per cent of global executives reported recent business transformations with which they were most familiar had a 'completely' or 'mostly' successful impact on performance.

(There are many different 'change programme' models out there that are commonly applied. They all underline the critical importance of 'communications', which in practice usually means 'exhortation'. If this is common to all change programme designs, could that be one of the reasons why so many fail? Exhortation is a classic aspect of top-down-driven change programmes.)

INCREASING PRESSURE TO ACHIEVE SUCCESSFUL, FUNDAMENTAL CHANGE

Given the poor experiences of most senior managers with profound business change initiatives and the growth of IT outsourcing and (more recently) business process outsourcing, many must be tempted to become cynical and concentrate on what they know they can do well.

VIEWS AND CLUES

The study quashes the myth that those in the most senior positions in the workplace are more likely to suffer from stress and other illnesses. Though there was shown to be a strong relationship between health and employment status, it is those in the lower grades of employment who are at far more risk of both physical and mental illness. The more senior you are in the employment hierarchy, the longer you are likely to live. In particular danger are workers who face high demands but have little control over their work, regardless of the 'type' of person they are. The study highlights employer and manager support as one way to reduce sickness absence.

Source: *Whitehall II study,* September 2004

(Author's Note: A police study demonstrated the absolute truth of this. The only change made in two police divisions (which were broadly similar, apart from high rates of sickness and absenteeism in one and low rates in the other) was to swap the two divisional commanders. The high rate went low and the low rate went high!)

In theory and in practice, hierarchy doesn't work, and no one put the reason better then GE's Jack Welch, himself an iconic manager. Hierarchy, he said, defines an organisation in which people have 'their face towards the CEO and their ass towards the customer'. The more charismatic the executive, and the more centralized the power, the more perverse the effect.

Source: *Why fearless leaders are something to dread, The Observer,* 6 May 2007

Increasingly though, this 'easy life' is not an option. As well as the expected pressures from competitors and from new government directives/initiatives, senior managers – at least in the private sector – are becoming increasingly wary of the growth of private equity funds. Despite the complications intrinsic in tax breaks, credit crunches and leveraging high levels of debt, the real message to established senior executives is simply, 'We can run your business better than you can ... or better than you *dare*!'

Similarly, as the track record of failure with public sector reform grows, so will the temptation to replace failing public sector managers with managers from the private sector. In all likelihood, however, these new brooms from a faster-moving, more innovative culture will still not have the key capabilities to bring effective change to the workplace. New ideas certainly ... new enthusiasm and energy probably ... but really new change implementation skills? Unlikely!

THE 'COVER YOUR BACK' STRAITJACKET

It is not at all surprising that many senior executives seek to cover their perceived inadequacies with 'tokens of success' as well as with more objective performance achievements through higher profits or improved, measurable service levels.

These tokens of success take the form of many acronyms and phrases, ranging from ISO 9000 through EFQM-type awards to customer service excellence charter marks and Investor in People awards. Each of these worthy initiatives doubtless has merit, but the temptation for beleaguered executives to invest them with a greater significance is obvious.

Equally, senior managers experience pressure to 'have an answer to potential criticisms'. They, in turn, pressurize their subordinates to meet imposed targets of performance, which may lead to false reporting upwards – as the pressure increases so does the temptation to tell your bosses what they want to hear, rather than what is really going on.

Most significantly, the combined pressures to succeed lead to decision inertia – 'If I can't be sure of succeeding, it's not worth attempting the change – I could be vulnerable.'

One of the most profound comments overheard during a discussion between outsourcing professionals was, 'They would never have got this far without outsourcing – they just do not have the nerve to go through the pain barrier themselves.'

Outsourcing was once seen by executives under pressure as a magic bullet for many of their woes. 'Let the professional service providers solve our most difficult operational problems, so that we can really focus on running the business and planning for an even more successful future.' But as questions are raised about the value of the whole outsourcing experience and management publications report a growing trend towards in-sourcing – there are now few hiding places for managers leading failed change programmes.

THE NEED FOR A NEW SOLUTION TO THE CHANGE QUAGMIRE

As the gloss comes off IT and business process outsourcing, the old pressures return once again to haunt senior managers in both public and private sectors. 'In our heart of hearts we know that we are not good at making fundamental day-to-day changes in the way that our organizations operate – but if outsourcing is more and more problematic, and the pressures on us to deliver results are growing ever stronger, what do we do now?'

Is it possible to improve the outsourcing experience in the future or are we only putting 'sticking plaster' over the gaping wounds that will never go away?

VIEWS AND CLUES

'You can get a lot more done with a kind word and a gun, than with a kind word alone.'

Al Capone

Rob Goffee, Professor of Organizational Behaviour at London Business School, advocates authentic leadership in his book 'Why Should Anyone Want to be Led by You?' He says that workplaces are full of cynical, disaffected followers who want leaders who inspire and excite. 'People are fed up with being worked, they are fed up of management fads and want to be led by real people they can trust.'

Source: *How leaders manage, The Times,* 31 May 2007

Employee resistance was ranked as the No. 1 obstacle to change initiatives in a recent survey by the Society for Human Resource Management, which received 403 responses from human resources professionals.

Yet the very people leading the change are not always effective at bringing it about. Leadership assessment research has found that executives at the vice president level and above are lacking in the skills necessary to oversee major shifts. Just 38 per cent of 2180 respondents in research by BlessingWhite say those executives are effective at managing change.

Source: *Employees react differently to company change, Newsday,* 13 May 2007

Perhaps we need a new solution to this change quagmire? Perhaps even a new model of how we can make effective business and organizational change in future? We definitely need to improve 'leadership'.

Managers are even worse at changing business 'culture'

Culture change is all about changing the way that people behave in the work environment – not just what they do but the way that they do it – and it is not easy. Identical processes and systems can be used by different groups across organizations to deliver very different levels of service to their stakeholders. A stakeholder (say a person from another part of the organization or a member of the public) knows very rapidly whether your organizational culture is essentially pleasant, helpful and efficient or just a hassle to deal with. And this depends primarily on your culture, rather than on your processes, systems and levels of formal staff training.

Traditionally, cultural change initiatives have been based on cultural measurements, gap analysis, 'training' presentations/facilitated workshops, annual assessment feedback and some managers leading by example – plus, of course, the old exhortation routine. Over time, more comprehensive approaches have been tried that link real rewards/promotions to appropriate 'new culture' behaviours. These are sometimes combined with an ongoing positive reinforcement of desired behaviours using a variety of guides/mentors in the work environment.

However, the end results of all these efforts are usually unsatisfactory to a greater or lesser degree, with even the most successful transitions taking several years to become established. Old habits and behaviours tend to persist despite changes in organization, processes, systems and 'new culture' support/rewards. Organizations that have been built up through mergers and acquisitions often have multiple cultures operating in parallel. These cultures reflect the cultures of the original component parts from which the current organization has been built.

If senior managers are poor at driving effective business change, they are even worse at implementing real day-to-day culture change. Most studies show failure rates for culture change initiatives running at about 90 per cent.

The change battleground is 'local'

Change failure is not usually due to *overt* 'change blockers' in the organization, although most change professionals have come across them from time to time. The causes of failure are much more insidious and can be best described as 'death by a thousand cuts' where opposition or indifference is experienced in small ways in many parts of the organization. Bit by bit, the proposed changes

---

VIEWS AND CLUES

There are three important things to remember about the life of French General Jean Martinet.

1. *He was a strict disciplinarian. He drilled his men brutally and demanded rigid adherence to the rules. He was so severe and exacting, he earned a place in the dictionary. Today, anyone displaying this style of leadership is branded 'a martinet'.*

2. *At the battle of Duisberg in 1776, General Martinet was shot dead by his own men.*

3. *What General Martinet failed to realize, and what we can all learn from his experience, is that leadership is a two-way street. Effective leadership depends on other people. It is their willingness to accept leaders and support them that makes effective leadership possible.*

Source: *Leadership is a two-way street*, Denis Bourne, *Magus Toolbox*, January 2000

The problem is that command and control seems to work, after a fashion. Because we are inside it, we do not see the enormous waste of time, effort and money that it imposes. We shrug off its obvious imperfections as normal – 'that's just the way it is'. There is therefore little cause to question whether it could be bettered. Moreover, command and control is ubiquitous. Its associated norms are rarely, if ever, challenged.

Source: John Seddon, *Freedom from Command and Control*, Vanguard Press, 2003

Poor management is rife in the UK workplace, with more than nine in 10 employees reporting that they have worked for a bad manager, research reveals.

The survey of 1500 UK staff, by law firm Eversheds, also shows that more than a quarter of workers believe management styles have become too harsh during the past year, with almost 50 per cent admitting that they have worked for a bully.

The study shows a lack of communication skills among UK managers. The overwhelming majority of workers (97 per cent) would like their bosses to communicate more clearly and directly.

Source: *Bad management is widespread in the UK*, Personneltoday, 10 May 2006

get delayed and diluted. Traditional top-down programme and project management almost always fails to address this type of insidious erosion.

The only effective way to address this dispersed, erosive threat is to engage significant numbers of leaders (influencers) selectively and use them to enhance rather than dilute proposed changes: winning hearts and minds of colleagues along the way. This principle applies to all continuous improvement programmes as well as major change initiatives. The trouble is that very few organizations (or consultants!) know how to identify dispersed informal leaders accurately.

Command and control is really just 'shallow' leadership

The vast majority of organizations, even today, are driven by command and control thinking. We have got used to top-down hierarchies; we separate decision making from work activities; we require managers to make decisions with tools such as budgets, targets, activity measures and so on. We tell people what to do, how to behave, and then check up often to ensure compliance. In particular, managers are 'taught' how to manage people, as well as budgets and targets. These are the fundamentals that make up 'command and control' management.

Research over the years has shown that command and control management is both very expensive – think of all the time, energy, political infighting and numerous tedious meetings associated with the whole budgeting process – and it inhibits the inherent talent and innovation potential that is buried beneath the surface within most organizations.

The overall impact of command and control management, however, is not easy to assess. Many structural changes are within the exclusive gift of the senior executive team. Takeovers/mergers, high-level changes in organization structure, new product development through established processes, geographic relocations, and quite extensive staff reductions can all usually be implemented with apparent success by management decree. It is only when staff behaviours and ways of working need to change significantly as part of a broader business change that the limits of executive power become very apparent. Often, the strategic decisions made by senior managers are very logical and compelling – the devil is in the detail. There is almost always a yawning gap between strategy and practical workplace implementation.

A number of consultancies and advanced organizations have made some progress in addressing the strategy/implementation divide by seeking to develop new leadership styles in management teams. These approaches take different forms but all aim to retain command and control capabilities for when these are needed – for example, to make strong, rapid decisions in a crisis – while also enabling a more inclusive style that encourages employee engagement, flexibility and innovation. The essence of this form of leadership training is to encourage managers at all levels to exhibit the behaviours associated with different management styles in appropriate situations. For example, in the set of management styles shown in Figure 1.2 in the two-by-two matrix, managers are encouraged to adopt a collaborative style most of the

---

VIEWS AND CLUES

'It has taken us years, and I think we are still not sure if we are getting things right even after substantial reengineering projects, a move to teams, new HR practices, two acquisitions, and a ton invested in technology. By now we should have reduced costs and created a more nimble company without a focus on hierarchy or fiefdoms. But it's tough to ensure that this is really happening. Most of us in this room have thousands of people we are accountable for stretched across the globe. It's impossible to manage or even know what's going on in the depths of the organisation. I mean, each of us can fool ourselves into thinking we're smart and running a tight ship. But really the best we can do is create a context and hope that things emerge in a positive way, and this is tough because you can't really see the impact your decisions have on people. So you just kind of hope what you want to happen is happening and then sound confident when telling others.'

Executive vice president, commercial lending

Source: *The Hidden Power of Social Networks*, Harvard Business School Press, 2004

'While the informal structure was undoubtedly important in the traditional organization, today it dominates.'

Source: J Champy, N Nohria, *Fast Forward*, Harvard Business School Press, 1996

In a recent survey conducted for Katzenbach, a third of the 390 respondents – all of them working at large US companies – admitted ignoring the rules when they found a better way to get things done. And in companies where managers worked closely with informal employee networks, respondents were three times more likely to describe their job environment as positive. The upshot: going by the book is not always the way to get results.

Source: *The hidden workplace, Fortune*, 18 July 2007.

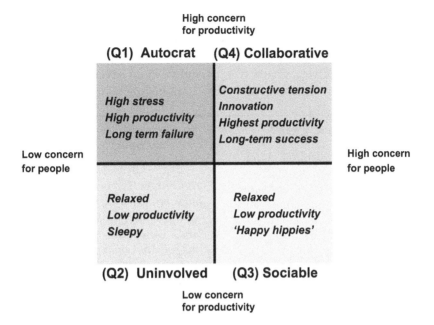

Figure 1.2   Examples of leadership styles

time, with an autocratic style (say) for crises, and the other styles only (if at all) on more social occasions.

As with many management techniques, however, adopting appropriate leadership styles for relevant situations within your organization is only part of the solution. Certainly, there is little evidence that enhanced leadership styles by themselves can impact on profound business change success rates. Nevertheless, appropriate leadership styles are a positive ingredient in collaborative working and an important move away from rigid, inflexible command and control.

Very few organizations have yet moved on to recognize and respond to the realities of human behaviour in work environments. In the real world, there is an entire spectrum of leaders spread across every organization.

Some informal leaders influence the views of many people and some of just one or two, influencing and 'leading' at all levels across your organization. The CEO, senior management team and all of the formal management hierarchy put together can identify less than a third of these 'leaders' and the management team's combined power to influence represents less than 20 per cent of the total potential influencing capability across all employees. Experience shows that this is pretty close to 'the real world' in most organizations.

From this perspective, it becomes possible to design the ways that people work in organizations very differently. It is even possible to achieve very high levels of effective change in both major change programmes and continuous improvement initiatives. There will be much more collaborative working between managers, influencers and those with key personal networks in this

---

VIEWS AND CLUES

Most large corporations have dozens if not hundreds of informal networks, which go by the name of peer groups, communities of practice, or functional councils – or have no title at all. These networks organize and reorganize themselves and extend their reach via cell phones, Blackberries, community Web sites, and other accessories of the digital age. As networks widen and deepen, they can mobilize talent and knowledge across the enterprise. They also help to explain why some intangible-rich companies, such as ExxonMobil and GE, have increased in scale and scope and boast superior performance.

Source: *Harnessing the power of informal employee networks, The McKinsey Quarterly 2007, Number 4*

According to the Chartered Management Institute, which published its 2007 Quality of Working Life report last week, the most commonly experienced management styles in the UK are bureaucratic (the experience of 40 per cent of respondents), reactive (37 per cent) and authoritarian (30 per cent), while just 17 per cent of the 1500 managers polled experienced management as innovative, 15 per cent as trusting and 13 per cent as entrepreneurial.

These averages hide huge differences in perception: what directors and senior managers saw as accessible, empowering and consensual, junior ranks judged bureaucratic (half the sample), reactive (38 per cent) and authoritarian (40 per cent).

Source: *Command, control...and you ultimately fail, The Observer, 16 December 2007*

In his book 'Good to Great' Jim Collins headed a research team to look at what drives average organizations to take a great leap and become great. The research concluded that a crucial component of greatness is a group of leaders with a paradoxical blend of personal humility and professional will. These leaders who Collins describes as Level 5 leaders channel their ambition away from themselves into the larger goal of building a great company. All of the companies in the study that went from good to great had Level 5 leadership in key positions, including the CEO, at the pivotal time of transition.

Source: *Leadership formation and Level 5 Leadership, Bob Calkin, amazines.com, 4 November 2007*

new organizational world. The collaboration will not be universal – it's just impractical for managers to collaborate with everyone. Once we know who the key players are across informal networks it becomes possible to implement practical, effective 'deep' leadership – the fruitless search to develop 'super managers' is replaced by practical leadership through 'super networks'. The real super managers are then those who can best engage and focus key individuals across the leadership super network.

In the meantime, you are stuck with tweaking your command and control organization. Effective leadership through 'super networks' is almost within your grasp. But for now, you must start by recognizing that command and control is really just 'shallow' leadership – it's achieving less than 20 per cent of your organization's leadership potential.

Chapter summary

Across both the private and public sectors there is a consistent, endemic failure of business leadership. This failure is highlighted by low (typically about 30 per cent) success rates for significant business change initiatives. Culture change initiatives perform even more poorly – with typical 10 per cent success levels. There is a yawning gap between business strategy and effective implementation. The dominant reason for these failures is the very real difficulty experienced in engaging key employees to drive change in a consistent and effective way across the organization and through to key external stakeholders.

Paradoxically, leadership failure is strongly associated with command and control management. Although 'strong' command and control management can be very effective in rapid decision making or dealing with a short-term crisis, 'deep' leadership – engaging natural leaders across an organization – is usually essential for effective implementation of profound business change that impacts on day-to-day work practices. Managers are typically very poor at identifying these natural leaders at all levels in an organization.

Although enhanced leadership styles for managers are an important enabling step towards deep leadership, these techniques will not by themselves solve the fundamental failures of traditional top-down business leadership.

Until natural local leaders (influencers and those with extensive personal networks) across an organization are harnessed to drive and implement profound changes, even restyled command and control managers will struggle to make a real leadership impact in changing times. Practical, effective 'deep' leadership through 'super networks' of central and local leaders is almost within your grasp. Currently, command and control management is really just 'shallow' leadership – it's achieving less than 20 per cent of your organization's full leadership potential.

The Importance of Influencers

Faced with high failure rates in major business change programmes, innovative consultants over recent years have developed influencer-based approaches to address the shortcomings of traditional top-down project management. These influencer engagement approaches started off as quite crude indicators of which staff influence their colleagues and might therefore be useful as change agents. Starting in the late 1990s, however, these primitive beginnings have evolved into quite sophisticated, relatively accurate assessments.

The reality of formal and informal leadership

A business organization is made up of many distributed leaders (influencers). Despite the (false) assumptions behind 'command and control management', there is not a single or small group of leaders but a whole spectrum of them (see Figure 2.1). Some leaders influence the views of many people and some of

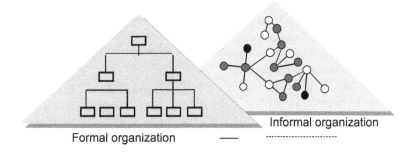

Formal organization   ——   Informal organization

Note: There is some overlap between the formal organization and informal (shadow) influence networks. Although there are exceptions, the trends are usually striking. Senior managers score poorly as influencers at lower levels – it is unusual to have many executive influencers. The lower down the hierarchy a manager is, the more likely he or she is to be a strong influencer of colleagues. Equally, a strong influencer who is by nature change positive is more likely to make a good first line manager, particularly during periods of change. Most of the key influencers are found at (non-manager) senior operational levels, associated with at least five years in the organization and consistent, above average work performa

Figure 2.1   Formal and natural leaders – the twin keys to change success

just one or two, influencing and 'leading' at all levels through their personal networks across your organization.

Who are the key influencers?

Between 5 and 10 per cent of all employees typically have the potential to make a real, positive difference to the success or failure of business change initiatives. These key individuals influence strongly enough to have a significant impact on the views of their colleagues, while also being change-positive by nature, or at least open-minded on change. Experience shows that in medium-sized or large organizations, each of the key influencers

---

DEFINITIONS

'Influencers' *are defined as:* *'People who can, because of their knowledge, skills and character and not their position, influence the views of multiple colleagues (typically peers and subordinates, and – sometimes – their managers) relating to significant business issues.*

'Key influencers' *are those influencers who wield greatest personal influence across the shadow organisation, and can (usually in collaboration with others of similar influence) have a major – positive or negative – impact on both the pace and direction of business change.*

'Executive influencers' *are influencers who happen to be in positions of formal authority (typically at board or very senior management levels).*

'Middle management influencers' *are influencers who happen to be in positions of formal authority in middle management levels.*

'First line management influencers' *are influencers who happen to be in positions of formal authority at first line management levels (typically supervisors or team leaders).*

'Local influencers' *are those (non-management) influencers whose influence primarily impacts on their specific, local work colleagues.*

'Change-positive influencers' *are those influencers (at any organizational level) who are by nature change-positive and broadly in favour of current proposed changes.*

'Open-minded influencers' *are those influencers (at any organizational level) who by nature often fall into the 'undecided' category regarding change. They are neither innovators nor change blockers, but can often sway the balance of opinion on change in particular business areas.*

'Change-negative influencers' *are those influencers (at any organizational level) who are by nature change-negative and broadly against current proposed changes. This opposition to change is often hidden, rather than blatant.*

'Change agents' are those individuals who are both influential and change-positive by nature (or at least open-minded on change) and active in supporting current change initiatives. (Note that many change-positive, would-be change agents are not change agents at all because of their lack of influence with colleagues).

'Stakeholder management' is the application of change management to specific stakeholder groups. Different stakeholder groups will typically be impacted differently by proposed changes, and change in each group will often need to be handled differently.

'Iterative samples' are samples of staff opinion based on the views of specific groups of influencers, rather than being representative of all staff. The views of change-positive influencers and open-minded influencers are used to identify additional individuals with these characteristics.

'People with extensive personal networks' or 'highly-connected individuals' are those with lots of links to colleagues or external individuals as identified during organizational network analysis (ONA) exercises. They are almost always good communication channels. Many but not all of these individuals will also be influencers.

influences on average about 20 colleagues or external contacts. Generally, there are significantly more open-minded influencers than change-positive influencers. Equally, there are usually significantly more open-minded influencers than change-negative influencers. Consequently, success or failure in business change often rests on the effective engagement (and winning the hearts and minds) of open-minded influencers. Only by convincing many of these key open-minded individuals can a practical tipping point for staff acceptance of change be reached.

The most intractable difficulties encountered in leading today's business change often result from some combination of the following, *very awkward,* people traits:

- Individuals and groups have limits in their capacity to absorb change – exceed the limits and people cease to function effectively.

- People look to their natural leaders/ influencers (often locally) in times of change, and these people are often not their supervisors/ managers/directors.

- Rumours abound in a business change climate – the tendency is towards extreme doom and gloom, particularly in the early stages.

- Executive directives (and exhortations) have limits in being able to make business change work – senior managers can usually stop change happening but they need a broad local consensus for effective implementation.

- Some people will always resist change – guessing who in advance is not easy; the larger the number of natural leaders who resist, the less likely the change is to work.

- Bandwagon effects are commonplace in business change – these can be both positive and negative.

- Management seniority is often inversely proportional to an understanding of business processes, systems, culture and relationships.

As mentioned earlier, change failure is not usually due to *overt* 'change blockers' in the organization. The causes of failure are much more insidious and can be best described as 'death by a thousand cuts' where opposition or indifference is experienced in small ways in many parts of the organization. Bit by bit, the proposed changes get delayed and diluted. Sometimes this erosion process is covertly assisted and accelerated by a few very influential change blockers. The only effective way to address this dispersed, erosive threat is to selectively engage significant numbers of dispersed leaders (influencers) and use them to enhance rather than dilute proposed changes, winning hearts and minds of colleagues along the way. This principle applies to all continuous improvement programmes as well as major change initiatives (see Figure 2.2).

How can influencers be used to lead successful business change?

By focusing on (and engaging) key change-positive and open-minded influencers throughout the organization, all these very awkward human traits can be harnessed and used to generate a bandwagon effect in favour of the desired business changes. The methods used to engage key influencers to lead all types of business change are discussed in Chapter 6 – Managing your business using informal employee networks.

The use of influencer-led approaches to change is totally compatible with all the main programme and project management methods. The bottom line is

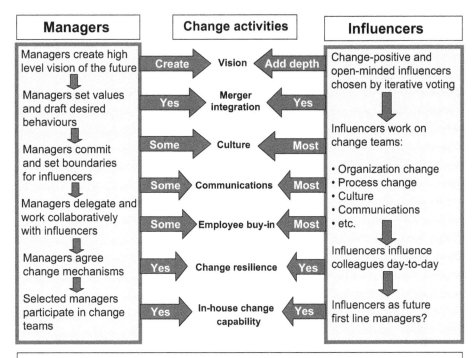

Change-positive and open-minded influencers (together with highly-connected individuals across informal networks) are the most effective channel for all types of business change that impact on employees – as shown above. Managers who engage with this type of informal network will become much more successful in achieving timely and effective change objectives – for both continuous change and for major change programmes – building change resilience and capability for the future.

Figure 2.2   Helicopter view of influencer engagement process

that you end up with very different people working in your change teams, with much more effective outputs.

By confronting the people difficulties mentioned above head-on, some business 'turnaround' specialists/company doctors move from business to business and achieve levels of success that defy the 70 per cent failure odds – usually in very difficult circumstances – without using influencers. Almost without exception, these specialists insist on the power to make product, financial *and people* changes, and then use this power to great effect in all areas. One of the most distinctive characteristics of these business saviours is not just that they reduce staff numbers – which they often but not always do – but that they make very selective changes at both executive and middle management levels. These changes are typically designed to replace a failed board and to substitute change agents for potential resistors in the middle ranks. Often, the end results closely resemble 'green field' management teams – which explains much of traditional company doctors' success, since green field organizations are generally better at implementing new ways of working than established businesses.

Unfortunately, these exercises are usually carried out using very blunt approaches based on assumptions that wholesale changes are always necessary, irrespective of the cultural scarring and staff disillusion that frequently results.

Such radical, and often unfocused, people changes at the top and upper-middle core of a business can often represent serious 'overkill'. The history of downsizing shows that high levels of redundancy, particularly in the middle management ranks, can lead to gaps in essential business knowledge and to many symptoms of organizational trauma – insecurity, low morale, low work quality, high turnover of skilled staff and a decreased ability to absorb further change. In a professionally run business change programme, one of the most important aspects to manage is the balance between essential staff changes (that facilitate important business changes) and the dangers of trauma (resulting from excessive staff changes, both internal reorganizations and through redundancy). In this important area, identifying valuable influencers plus positive individuals with extensive personal networks across the organization will rapidly and clearly highlight the people that you need to *retain* if the business is not to be profoundly damaged.

By focusing on influencers and informal personal networks throughout the organization, you can achieve this essential balance without risking the extremes of change doctor 'overkill' or the 'under-kill/wishful thinking' associated with traditional 'soft and fluffy' – communicate with everyone and hope for the best – change management. Soon, the most successful change doctors will also be using influencers to lead business change.

Almost all major business change programmes over the last decade and more have used some combination of 'formal' change management techniques and activities. No experienced change specialist really doubts that most of the traditional techniques (sponsors, senior management presentations, question and answer sessions, in-house publications, model offices, staff involvement, behaviours training, feedback mechanisms, and so on) are useful and many are probably essential.

Yet the failure rate in business change exceeds 70 per cent, particularly when rigorous comparisons with the main initial programme objectives are made. You will not be surprised to hear that recent research reveals that by far the biggest factor in these failures is the people factor – way ahead of 'unclear visions' and 'technology difficulties' in change projects of the late 1990s/early 2000s.

Traditional change management techniques have missed something fundamental about people factors. Only in recent years have we been able to identify this missing link and develop techniques to effectively address it.

Put simply, this change management missing link can be summarized as follows:

- The (designed) formal management organization determines the overwhelming majority of day-to-day activities and operational decisions. The formal organization holds sway right across all routine aspects of the business, from operations staff and accountants, through to IT technicians and sales staff. (Organizational *design* is about providing stability, predictability and repeatability – the exact opposite of what transpires through any change process.)

- A shadow organization of influencers and those with extensive personal networks (with typically a 60 per cent+ mismatch to the formal management structure) largely determines *the scope and pace of change* in the way that the business operates. Communication between this shadow organization and formal management is usually heavily distorted by personal and group 'politics'.

- Only when change-positive balances of opinion exist in *both* the formal senior management organization and in the informal 'key influencer' organization can (people-disruptive) change be successfully implemented.

- Where the shadow and formal organizations come into conflict in a change situation, the balance of influence in the shadow organization will almost always win the day .... or force an exhausting and indeterminate draw.

Therefore in any people-disruptive change programme, change management mechanisms are needed to effectively cover both the formal management of the business and the informal influencer-driven 'shadow' organization. However, the accurate identification of change-positive (and open-minded) influencers is far from obvious!

How do you identify the key influencers?

Although many traditional change methods have involved influencers to some degree, these have almost always failed to recognize the importance of accuracy during the influencer identification process. The most common way of identifying influencers to act as change agents or project sponsors is to 'ask the change team and ask the relevant managers'. But as change projects stall, falter and fail, few of those involved ever notice that they have typically only identified one third or less of the influencers available – and they have probably included several change blockers who will often act as trojan horses, slowing things up and generally making life difficult. (Full staff sampling and representative sampling are also highly inaccurate in identifying the change-positive and open-minded influencers.)

The best influencer identification techniques started off by using an iterative interview/group meetings process (see Figure 2.3 and Figure 2.4) to progressively identify and rank influencers according to their scope and weight of influence. During this process, care is taken to identify:

- those individuals who are both influential and change-positive by nature;

- those individuals who are both influential and open-minded by nature.

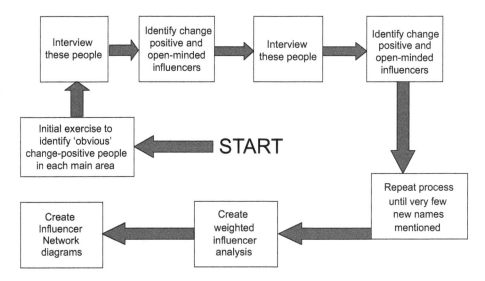

Note: Only the change-positive and open-minded people participate

Figure 2.3   Accurately identify change-positive and open-minded influencers

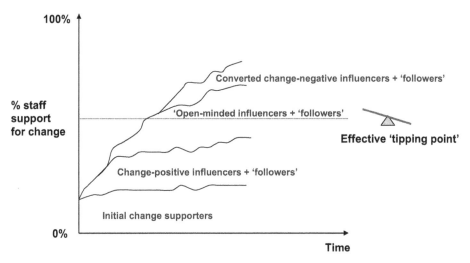

Figure 2.4   Typical anatomy of a change 'bandwagon'

These two groups of influencers form the 'raw materials' for the selective use of both influencers and managers (some managers are influential and others not) during all change projects that impact significantly on people in their work environment. The progressive use of influence in business change is illustrated in Figure 2.5.

During the influencer identification process about 20 per cent of the relevant employee population typically become involved. While all of these individuals will have been identified at least once as a potential change-positive or open-minded influencer, some will score much more heavily then others during the iterative 'voting' process. Once this part of the exercise is complete, the highest-scoring influencers are provisionally selected and reviewed by a relevant senior management team. This allows senior managers to eliminate any individuals who they believe could potentially be negative or disruptive. (Great care should be taken to minimize the impact of personal biases – after all, senior managers have a poor understanding of local influencers and are likely to be surprised by many of the choices.) In particular, they will focus on those who might be experiencing significant health or relationship problems that could impede their effectiveness as change agents. This senior management review is an important element in building management buy-in to the influencer engagement process.

More recently, this iterative logic has been applied to 100 per cent or representative samples of employees by using software-based questionnaires that generate 'opinion networks'. These database networks show 'who identified whom' as influential change agents. The outputs can then be subanalyzed to

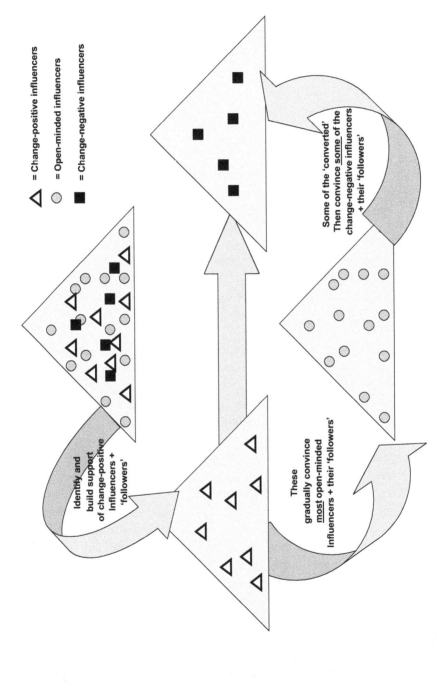

Figure 2.5   Gaining support for business change – progressively through influencers

identify only those candidates who were named as a result of network 'threads' that originated from known change-positive individuals. This replaces the manual process described above, but a senior management review of those selected is still necessary.

Because the best influencer identification techniques concentrate heavily on accuracy in identifying influencers, traditional measures such as psychometric tests and representative staff opinion surveys have been rejected as being too inaccurate. Psychometrics measure individual characteristics outside of the specific work/change context and representative staff surveys are biased by including the views of both the indifferent and the outright change blockers. Indeed, it is only by carrying out an accurate identification of influencers that the errors in other methods become crystal clear. The opinions of managers (even local managers) are often limited as they readily identify those who influence upwards, but not sideways and downwards to their colleagues. Similarly, individuals with large personal networks (see Chapter 3) should not be assumed to be influential, although many are.

When carrying out an influencer identification exercise, some areas (particularly smaller areas) of the organization will sometimes be found to have no identified change-positive or open-minded influencers. These are called influencer 'cold spots'. Further work is then needed to identify the local individuals who could act as the best available (though not ideal) change agents in cold spot areas. Generally this is done by asking identified influencers to give their opinion on change-positive or open-minded individuals in cold spot areas even when these people are not particularly influential. This may be supplemented by identifying influencers outside cold spot areas who have been nominated as potential influential change agents by some of those within cold spot areas – and by running a separate organization network analysis to identify those with the most extensive personal communication networks in cold spot areas (see Chapter 3 – The importance of informal employee networks).

Indeed, the extent of the management misconceptions about who are the real change-positive and open-minded influencers is difficult to overestimate. Over the years, the author has used three landscape slides (see Figure 2.6) to highlight this issue. In the first slide, senior managers (who usually only identify between 5 and 15 per cent of these key influencers) see the influencer landscape as a flat desert with a few peaks where they see a few key influencers. In the second slide, local managers (including supervisors and team leaders) can identify up to a third of the real key influencers. They view the landscape as a series of hills and mountains but with quite extensive fog in many areas.

Senior management perceptions ➡ 5 to 15 % accuracy

First line management perceptions ➡ 20% to 30% accuracy

The reality

Note: On average only 40 per cent of first line managers are 'influencers'

Figure 2.6   Distortion of the influencer 'landscape'

Only when a full influencer identification exercise is carried out can the full influencer landscape be seen – with very little fog.

One interesting element of an influencer analysis is to see what percentage of local first-line managers (including supervisors and team leaders) fall into the change-positive or open-minded influencer categories. On average, the figure is only about 40 per cent – so that most first line managers are either not influential with their subordinates or are by nature change-negative! In our experience, the percentage of first line managers who are also change-positive or open-minded influencers varies widely from about 20 to 70 per cent, so take care before assuming that the 40 per cent average applies to your organization.

Interestingly, these findings correlate well with likely success or failure in change initiatives. In one particular back office organization operating across two sites, one site with 70 per cent of local managers being key positive/open-minded influencers required a minimum of change management support during a major transformation exercise. In contrast, the other site – with a much lower ratio of change-positive managers – required extensive interventions before major changes could be successfully made. This included changing more than half of all first line managers (as part of a broader technology-based reorganization) and replacing them largely with selected key influencers.

Overall, the most desirable pattern of selected dispersed leaders is that there are very few senior managers (due to delegation and reduced day-to-day contact with large groups of employees); a somewhat higher percentage of middle managers for similar reasons; and many supervisors/team leaders (why would you *not* want your supervisors/team leaders to be both influential with colleagues and change-positive or at least open-minded on change?) Non-managers will nevertheless dominate, typically representing at least 70 per cent of identified dispersed leaders (see Figure 2.7).

The patterns found in a particular organization can be used as key inputs into short-term management interventions (training, mentoring, staff rotation) and ongoing succession planning.

Winning hearts and minds across managers and influence networks

Before driving ahead with the use of selected influencers, it is important to win the hearts and minds of those who will often not feature strongly at all in the lists of influencers – namely the managers. The concept of empowering influencers is often alien to many managers' instincts and may be viewed as a personal criticism (why am I not influential?) or a threat to future career prospects. In practice, after an initial reality check, most senior and middle managers recognize the power of the influencer approach and recognize the logic of their (usually) lowly position in the influence pecking order.

This logic, however, does not apply in the same way to local first line managers (including supervisors and team leaders). These individuals are faced with the bulk of the face-to-face management that occurs across the organization. Further, the fundamental logic of influencer engagement is that they should ideally be strong change-positive (or at least) open-minded influencers. Therefore an influence analysis exercise is likely to be perceived by local first line managers in one of three ways:

1. I am delighted because I have been identified as a strong change-positive (or open-minded) influencer. My future career prospects will be enhanced by more engagement.

2. I am discouraged and worried because I am relatively new to the organization and have not yet had a chance to become influential. This could be another hurdle in the way of my career progression.

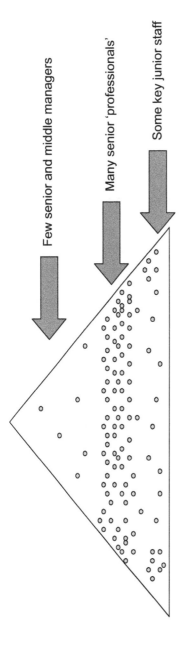

Few senior and middle managers

Many senior 'professionals'

Some key junior staff

○ = Identified strong influencer

Note: Most employees are influenced by specific colleagues who they work with on a day-to-day basis. Senior and middle managers are often respected but are not directly influential with most people in the workplace. The majority of change-positive and open-minded influencers fit into the category of senior professional workers – typically those who have been in their current jobs for 5+ years and are respected for their skills and capability, as well as having an 'influencing' personality. A minority (about 40%) of these will typically be local first line managers. Sometimes there are age boundaries to influence networks, where some individuals (say) at more junior levels will strongly influence their younger peers but not those who are older or have been with the organisation longer. Influence boundaries are often correlated with historical events, such as mergers and acquisitions or with major recruitment events in the past.

Figure 2.7 Typical influencer patterns within organizations

3.   I am worried because I am an established local manager and have not been identified as a strong change-positive or open-minded influencer.

In practice, only the latter group of local managers need be concerned. If the organization persists with influencer engagement, their performance in their existing jobs will certainly come under scrutiny, particularly as influence becomes an important part of talent management and succession planning.

The underlying principle behind winning the support of colleagues for change initiatives is to progressively use influencers to win over their followers – those who they influence – in a logical sequence, starting with the easiest first. (An example of cross-site influence networks is given in Figure 2.8, with typical patterns of influencers building support being shown in Figure 2.9), Therefore the first choice of individuals to engage in a change team is relevant – those with

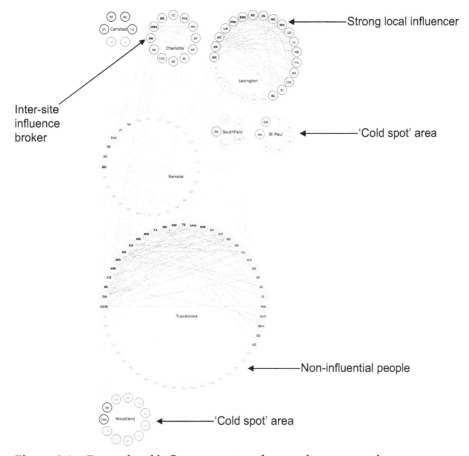

Figure 2.8   Example of influencer network overview across sites

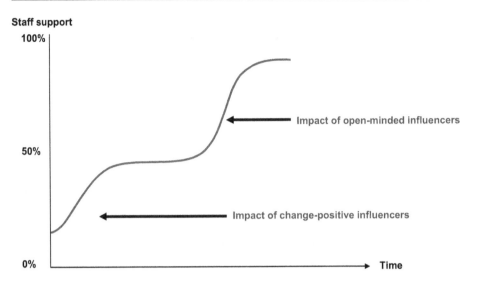

Staff support

Figure 2.9   Progressively building staff support for relevant change

knowledge of the areas impacted by the proposed change – change-positive influencers.

By engaging these key individuals and genuinely involving them in change decisions, the initial objective is to win their 'hearts and minds' in favour of the relevant changes. As a natural consequence of this support, their influence is then used (enhanced by appropriate meetings, social events, e-mails, videos and so on as necessary) to win the hearts and minds of the colleagues that they influence.

Following on from engagement of change-positive influencers (and sometimes in parallel with it), relevant open-minded influencers are also engaged to win their 'hearts and minds' in favour of the relevant changes. Wherever possible, priority is given to those who are influenced by one or more change-positive influencers and whose personal influence network is strong across relevant business areas to provide maximum influence 'coverage'. Once again, as a natural consequence of this support, their influence is then used (enhanced by appropriate meetings, social events, e-mails, videos and so on as necessary) to win the hearts and minds of the colleagues that they influence.

Many of the influencers engaged as described above (some of whom will be managers) will also have strong personal communication networks (indicated through ONA analysis, as described in Chapter 3). However, it will often be necessary and/or desirable to make use of other non-influential individuals with strong personal networks to ensure (as a minimum) that informal change project communications are highly effective. Unless these people are thought to be change-negative, they should be seriously considered as key components in a professional change communications plan.

Impact of influencer engagement on future leadership styles

A number of consultancies and advanced organizations have made progress in addressing the strategy/implementation divide by seeking to develop new leadership styles in management teams. These approaches take different forms but all aim to retain some command and control capabilities for the rare occasions when these are needed – for example, when strong, rapid decisions are essential in a crisis – while also enabling a more inclusive style that encourages employee engagement, flexibility and innovation on a day-to-day basis. Clearly, rigid command and control (autocratic) management styles fit very badly with the extensive cooperative approach needed for effective engagement of key influencers on a day-to-day basis.

Yet many, if not most, managers in organizations today feel that they need to adopt a dominant command and control management style most of the time. So how will management styles and behaviours need to change in future as the logic and practice of influencer engagement becomes widely accepted? Which managers will survive and thrive in this new, more collaborative work environment?

The most noticeable changes at each management level are likely to be as follows:

- Executives and senior managers will still need to get their strategic decisions right in a rapidly changing business environment. Indeed, for many top managers, clear strategic thinking and the ability to communicate key concepts in practical terms will become increasingly important. No longer do they need to dictate precisely *how* the strategy will be interpreted in detail or *how* it will be implemented. They will delegate more and more practical strategy interpretation and implementation work to informal leaders (some of whom will be managers) across their organizations. The most successful senior executives will be those who can make clear strategic decisions, combined with an ability to effectively communicate the practical essence of key strategies, without seeking to fill in all the details or to micro manage implementation.

VIEWS AND CLUES

CEO job tenure in the 1990s was shorter than it had ever been, as chief executives who failed to improve corporate bottom lines or to deliver on promises found themselves quickly removed from office. All of them, of course, enjoyed soft landings with their golden parachutes, but the fact that CEOs were treated as both superheroes and abject failures was telling. CEOs were shown the door with undue haste for the same reason that they were lavished with such attention: because they were expected to be miracle workers...

At any moment, of course, there are always CEOs with exceptional track records, executives who just seem better able to outthink their competitors, anticipate their customer market, and motivate their employees. But the business landscape of the last decade is littered with CEOs who went from being acclaimed as geniuses to being dismissed as fools because of strategic mistakes.......

As business professor Sydney Finkelstein, author of a fascinating study of corporate failure, wrote: 'CEOs should come with the same disclaimer as mutual funds: Past success is no guarantee of future success.'

Source: *The wisdom of crowds,* James Surowiecki, Abacus, 2004, pp. 217–219

The pitfalls of handing over power are almost as great for companies as they are for dictators. Yet, half the US chief executives questioned last October by the Centre For Creative Leadership, said their HR departments were making no contribution to developing new leaders.

At best, it is a damning indictment of the relationship between chief executives and HR. At worst, it is a damning indication that many HR departments aren't doing their job.

Source: *How to buy a CEO, Personnel today.com,* 4 March 2003

- Middle managers will form the essential 'glue' that understands clearly the key elements of the business strategy, interprets the strategy in practical (but not detailed) terms and collaborates with both peer and subordinate managers to create, inform and monitor effective and efficient change mechanisms. These change mechanisms will be driven primarily by informal leaders, namely change-positive and open-minded influencers across the organization. Command and control-style management will only be needed in rare crisis situations – where change implementation mechanisms are not working well or where strategy is being misinterpreted and views have become entrenched. The percentage of middle managers that are also influencers will increase significantly, although their most important influence networks will be focused on local managers who will become their direct reports and their peer middle managers across relevant organizational boundaries.

- Local, first line managers (such as supervisors and team leaders) will mostly be change-positive or open-minded influencers – the main exception being new local managers who have potential but who have not been with the organization (or group) long enough to create an effective influence network with colleagues and cross-organizational peers. These exceptions may include individuals with the potential to eventually move into middle or senior management positions, but who are going through a process of gaining practical operational experience (see Chapter 5 – Throwing out those tired old HR models). The management styles of these key influencers are naturally collaborative and will continue to be so in an environment of extensive influencer engagement.

As influencer engagement becomes more and more established as a natural component of modern business management, so collaborative management styles and good communication skills across all organizational levels will become increasingly important. Those individuals in management positions who have these capabilities will thrive, while those without them will progressively decline as pressures build for them to move within or outside the organization (by choice or necessity).

More women will become managers

Interestingly, the shift in management skills towards better collaborative and communication skills will have one important additional side effect. Over time, more and more managers will be women!

The reason for this trend is basic biology. Women's brains are designed in fundamentally different ways from men's brains where communication and effective collaboration are concerned.

In many ways, men – the primeval hunters – have evolved brain characteristics where a narrow focus on priorities, rapid decisions and testosterone-based aggressive behaviour lead to successful hunting and mating. These characteristics fit very well with command and control management styles and to a substantial degree explain why men dominate management positions in the business world today.

VIEWS AND CLUES

Even more impressive was an experiment performed recently at Innocentive, a spin-off of Eli Lilly, which set up an experimental (decision) market to test whether its employees could distinguish between drug candidates that were likely to be approved by the FDA and those that were likely to be rejected. Investing in potential drugs is among the most important decisions a pharmaceutical company can make, because its profits depend on maximising the number of successful drugs and minimising the number of unsuccessful drugs it develops. A reliable method of predicting in advance which drug candidates were likely to win FDA approval would therefore be tremendously valuable. Innocentive set up the experiment by devising realistic profiles and experimental data for six different drugs, three of which it knew would be approved and three it knew would be rejected. When trading opened on these drugs, the market – made up of a diverse mix of employees – quickly identified the winners, sending their prices soaring, while the losers' prices sank...

Decision markets are well suited to companies because they circumvent the problems that obstruct the flow of information at too many firms: political infighting, sycophancy, and a confusion of status with knowledge. The anonymity of the markets and the fact that they yield a relatively clear solution, while giving individuals an unmistakable incentive to uncover and act on good information, means that their potential value is genuinely hard to overestimate...

A relatively small group of diversely informed individuals making guesses about the likelihood of uncertain events produced, when their judgements had been aggregated, an essentially perfect decision. What more could a company want?

Source: *The wisdom of crowds*, James Surowiecki, Abacus, 2004, pp. 221–223

Winston Churchill once famously said: 'Never think that a small band of determined people can't change the world. Indeed it is the only thing that ever has.'

Yet as we look at organisational change, it always seems to be heralded as a major initiative, driven from the top by some champion with the express aim of making the organisation more effective, competitive, less vulnerable, quicker to respond, more product focused, more customer focused – the list is endless.

Chief executives have made their names by being change champions, but all the publicity overlooks a fundamental fact. None of the great and good could have done it without the support and commitment of a myriad of people throughout the organisation.

Source: *How to lead change from within*, *Personneltoday.com*, 13 March 2007

In contrast, women – the primeval gatherers – have evolved brain characteristics where the ability to consider many different issues at the same time and to communicate multiple concepts and views effectively leads to success. Food gathering and child rearing are best performed as collaborative activities and women have evolved these skills very effectively over time.

Therefore as the business world changes towards increased collaboration, influencer engagement and effective informal communication, women are strongly placed to play a much-increased role in management. Research to date suggests that women are already over-represented in informal influencer and communication networks relative to their male colleagues. Nevertheless, the trend towards more women managers will depend significantly on the make up of the local workplace population – large female workgroups tend to have more female managers and vice versa for men. As a rule of thumb, the increase in women managers is likely to be more marked at local and middle management levels, where collaborative and communication skills are more essential. Women will still have a significant challenge on their hands as they seek to enter the (predominantly) male bastions of the boardrooms in large organizations. Strategic decision making and crisis management will remain key executive responsibilities that fit the evolutionary male characteristics well. But the boardroom will still not be immune to the fundamental shifts in management styles, working culture and sexes occurring lower down the management hierarchy.

Harvesting the latent power of influencers

Influencers exist in all businesses. They inhabit most groups across the organization and hold a range of views on business change. Some influencers will by nature be change positive, some open minded and some broadly anti-change. Their influence networks will typically be widespread and varied – but largely unknown, even to the influencers themselves.

Many command and control managers challenge the idea that informal influence networks can be made to work on any consistent basis. They argue that since influence networks have existed for a long time, why have they not exerted their magic to help previous change initiatives? The answer in a sense is very obvious – the influence networks across and between organizations are generally in a latent state. No one has really tried to harness them consistently up to now.

Because most influencers tend to be open minded on change, the overall impact of influencers pulling in different directions (or none at all) in an uncoordinated way tends to be muted. From time to time, particular issues arise that activate either the change-positive or the change-negative influencers into action, as they seek to build support for or against particular initiatives. These efforts are generally inefficient, since influencers can typically only identify and focus on a fraction of their true influence networks. When the change-positive influencers succeed in convincing sufficient open-minded influencers and thereby a critical mass of their colleagues to support a particular change, the impact of their activities is often misinterpreted by management. Managers simply see staff acceptance and assume that the success is down to their hard work, good project management and their powers of persuasion! However, when change-negative influencers succeed in building a colleague consensus against change, the impact is far more visible. The resulting problems and failures are then attributed to poor project management or just a backward looking, change resistant workforce. The underlying skirmishes (and sometimes battles) across influence networks are lost in the fog of management misperceptions.

VIEWS AND CLUES

'We had an opportunity to compare nominated representatives with identified influencers during the implementation process. Overwhelmingly, influencers were the key to success.'

Tim Pink, Management of Change Manager, TITAN Change Programme, Nationwide Building Society

Source: *Change in our times*, Wentworth Management Programme, May 1999

In organisational life, influence is a key skill. It helps earn co-operation from colleagues, ensures your voice is heard and makes you a better leader. We all influence at minor levels every day without even knowing it, but step your influencing powers up a notch, and you'll begin to realise their career-building potential very quickly.

Remember that the real skill is learning how to influence through commitment, loyalty and trust, rather than through mere compliance or, at worst, coercion.

'At most organisational levels, "making things happen" depends as much on influencing sideways and upwards as it does on managing through the hierarchy,' says Ceri Roderick, assessment and development specialist at occupational psychologist Pearn Kandola. 'Change processes in particular are best achieved through influence rather than imposition.'

Source: *Influencing: How to develop your influencing skills*, Personneltoday, 25 January 2005

The real lessons are not learnt and future change successes and failures come almost as surprises, with managers either grabbing the glory or attributing blame as the situation demands.

It is only by accurately identifying influence networks and then engaging selected influencers to drive change that the largely inert power of influencers can be unleashed. The underlying battles between change-positive and change-negative influencers for the support of open-minded influencers will still take place. The forces for change will, however, be identified, coordinated and engaged in the change process – while the change-negative forces will continue to be uncoordinated and largely disorganized. (Even without the conscious use of influencers, some coordinated change activities can reveal the latent power of informal knowledge networks – see the power of 'decision markets' in Views and Clues.)

By using much more efficient change coordination mechanisms across influence networks, large and controversial change initiatives can be successfully implemented, even where the initial balance of employee opinion is change negative. Employee morale rises consistently every time that influence networks are used effectively. This is true even where initially controversial change has been implemented. These change coordination mechanisms are described in Chapter 6 – Managing your business using informal employee networks.

Chapter summary

The causes of change failure are insidious and can be best described as 'death by a thousand cuts' where opposition or indifference is experienced in small ways in many parts of the organization. Bit by bit, the proposed changes get delayed and diluted. Sometimes this erosion process is covertly assisted and accelerated by a few very influential change blockers. The only effective way to address this dispersed, erosive threat is to selectively engage significant numbers of dispersed leaders (influencers) and use them to enhance rather than dilute proposed changes, winning hearts and minds of colleagues along the way. This principle applies to all continuous improvement programmes as well as major change initiatives.

There are two categories of dispersed leaders that need to be identified and engaged in change activities. The first are those significant influencers who are 'by nature' positive in their attitudes to change. The second are those significant influencers who are 'by nature' open minded in their attitudes to change. The

VIEWS AND CLUES

With so many managers and professionals stuck at work, there is a growing consensus among management gurus that the stuck-at-work epidemic is symptomatic of a serious disorder in the organization of corporations. The problem, in a nutshell-to-go is this: Succeeding in today's economy requires lightning-fast reflexes and the ability to communicate and collaborate across the globe. Coming up with innovative ideas, products, and services means getting people across different divisions and different companies to work together. 'More and more value is created through networks,' says John Helferich, a top executive and former head of research and development at Masterfoods usa, a division of Mars Inc. and the maker of such products as M&Ms. 'The guys who are good at it are winning.'....

... There is hope, however, and the promise of at least partial liberation from the tyranny of time constraints. Why? Because the long-term interests of individuals and smart companies are aligned. To compete, successful corporations will have to make it easier and less time-consuming for their employees to collaborate. They will learn how to live with fewer time-sapping meetings and unnecessary feedback loops – or find themselves outrun by more nimble competitors. The eventual result: less frustration for knowledge workers. Moves in this direction are already under way as savvy companies analyze their internal social networks and identify bottlenecks. Intel Corp., for example, sees an opportunity in creating technology that lowers the time cost of teamwork. And others, such as Eli Lilly & Co., are providing more corporate support for both internal and external networks. 'It's a new mental model for how you run a company,' says McKinsey's Bryan. 'The winners will be those who can handle more complexity.'

Source: *The real reasons you're working so hard, BusinessWeek*, 3 October, 2005

In less than a generation, the social fabric of our workplaces has undergone a number of dramatic changes.

Now, chief executives come and go with alarming frequency, nobody believes in the notion of a job for life and union membership has slipped to around a third of the country's workers, with the average age of members rising fast. Meanwhile, all the evidence suggests a lack of trust in business leaders.

Working people no longer feel allegiances to the institutions that used to buttress working life. People do not commit themselves to formal social institutions in the way their parents did.

So what are they doing instead? They are getting together in more informal networks inside and outside the workplace. Analysis of how we are developing so-called 'social capital' reveals there is a trend towards the formation of loose types of associations – more personal and less visible social networks.

Source: *Making most of your employee networks, Personneltoday.com*, 10 June 2003

desired change-positive and open-minded leaders (influencers) cannot be accurately identified by psychometrics or any form of representative opinion sampling. (Attempts to identify influential change agents in this way will always get distorted by the inputs of change-negative or disaffected individuals across the organization.) The best influencer engagement techniques use iterative sampling (where a handful of individuals who are known for their change-positive views start an iterative process where only those change-positive and open-minded leaders who are identified at each stage can participate in the influential change agent identification process).

There are usually more open-minded leaders than change-positive leaders and achieving a tipping point in winning employee hearts and minds will usually require a substantial proportion of the open minded to buy in to proposed changes. The best techniques use change-positive leaders to convince the open minded through a process of focused engagement, change team building and selective mentoring.

The most desirable pattern of selected dispersed leaders is that there are very few senior managers (due to delegation and reduced day-to-day contact with large groups of employees), a slightly higher percentage of middle managers for similar reasons and many supervisors/team leaders. Non-managers nevertheless dominate, typically representing at least 70 per cent of identified dispersed leaders (see Figure 2.7).

Interestingly, the shift in management skills needed to make influencer engagement work – better collaborative and communication skills – will have one important additional side effect. Over time, more and more managers will be women!

It is only by accurately identifying influence networks and then engaging selected influencers to drive change that the largely inert power of influencers can be unleashed. The underlying battles between change-positive and change-negative influencers for the support of open-minded influencers will still take place. However, the forces for change will be identified, coordinated and engaged in the change process, while the change-negative forces will continue to be uncoordinated and largely disorganized.

The good news therefore is that leading influencer engagement techniques can profoundly improve your chances of successfully implementing both continuous and major change in your organization. It also enables very significant improvements in talent management at first line management levels.

Staff morale rises consistently because dispersed leaders are engaged, raising not only their own morale but also the morale of those many colleagues that they influence.

The Importance of Informal Employee Networks

Business change programmes in recent years have led to organizations with fewer levels of hierarchy and more flexible organizational boundaries. Organizational silos have been targeted again and again as major constraints to business efficiency and effectiveness. A by-product of these structural changes is that much effective work increasingly occurs through informal networks of interpersonal relationships, rather than through formal reporting structures or work processes. As a consequence, these invisible networks have become fundamental to performance and strategy execution.

Informal networks can be accurately identified and measured

In the last decade, in parallel with developments in leveraging influencers, mechanisms for measuring and analyzing informal communications that started life as social science questionnaire tools have been enhanced and adapted for the business world. Social Network Analysis is now Organizational Network Analysis (ONA).

ONA provides a pictorial scan of the informal organizational activities. It is a powerful means of making invisible patterns of informal communications flow, knowledge access and collaboration visible. Consulting firms and forward-thinking individuals in major businesses have flocked to ONA roundtable groups and conferences over the last few years. Organizations as diverse as Procter & Gamble, The American Heart Association, BAE Systems, BP, 3M, IBM, Lehman Brothers, Mars, Microsoft, NASA, Glaxo Smith Kline and Pfizer have all started exploring and (sometimes) implementing the benefits of ONA. Indeed, ONA is in danger of becoming fashionable. Unlike many previous management fashions, however, ONA has the potential to enable a step function change in business efficiency, innovation and overall effectiveness. In the process, it has the potential to change forever the ways that employees are managed, motivated, promoted and developed.

AVOIDING AND OVERCOMING PROBLEMS WITH QUESTIONNAIRE ACCURACY

First though, a few words of warning: ONA has one potentially very large Achilles Heel – the likely inaccuracies associated with all questionnaire-based methods seeking to extract accurate insights regarding sensitive information.

Most people are familiar with mass opinion surveys carried out by polling companies to compile surveys of voting intentions. These surveys (typically carried out frequently and with a sample size of more than 1000 people each) mostly have a good track record in predicting mass voter intentions to within a few percentage points. Nevertheless, even these very large, anonymous surveys have inbuilt inaccuracies – for example, they tend to underestimate the actual vote for right of centre parties and they can be volatile in predicting 'squeeze' effects resulting from tactical voting.

When questionnaires are used in work environments, inaccuracies can become very serious and even undermine the whole validity of the exercise. The reasons can be summarized under two main headings – fear and lethargy:

- Fear that if you give an accurate feedback, you will upset certain colleagues and/or that your response might upset your superior(s) and have a negative effect on your future career prospects. In 360-degree assessments, for example, providing honest feedback on your boss is widely regarded as being career inhibiting, particularly in smaller groups where even anonymous negative feedback can be easily attributed to a few 'likely culprits'.

- Lethargy, built on a combination of disinterest and pressure of 'more important things to do with my time'. A lack of credibility in many HR departments also has a negative effect on both questionnaire response rates and the care taken in completing HR-type surveys.

In one cultural survey for a large IT department, employees were asked to assess what percentage of their colleagues were consistently carrying out desired behaviours (helpful, flexible, innovative and so on) on a day-to-day basis. There was very little variation in the responses across different IT sections as an overall 70 per cent compliance figure was indicated from a 65 per cent response rate. Cause for some modest satisfaction? Not really! When a culture change group of 25 committed and representative change-positive and open-minded influencers completed the same survey, with a 100 per cent response, the overall compliance figure was 18 per cent with considerable variations across different IT sections. It took 6 months of hard work driven by managers and these key influencers before

The Indexer Questionnaire

Welcome and thank you for participating. Please read the directions carefully.

Each question is presented as a pair of statements, either one of which might be a perfect description of one, specific characteristic of your organisation. The two statements offered relate to observable processes and practices, as they might operate in your organisation.

It is possible, however, that the truth lies somewhere between the two extremes. Please note that the two extremes are not necessarily polar opposites. Please indicate where you believe your organisation lies, either at one of the extremes or somewhere in between, by clicking on the appropriate circular button:

Senior managers frequently ask questions about current or planned actions to improve output performance	○ ○ ○ ○ ○ ○	Senior managers frequently ask questions about recent or current results
Senior managers often talk with operational employees in their own workplace to find out their views	○ ○ ○ ○ ○ ○	Senior managers rarely visit the workplace, and when they do, other managers are usually with them
Procedures for recruiting additional staff require that customer service improvements are shown to get fast approval	○ ○ ○ ○ ○ ○	Procedures for recruiting additional people are slow and mostly require top level approval
Appraisal is frequent, irregular and focuses on output results delivered, occasionally being recorded in summary form	○ ○ ○ ○ ○ ○	Appraisal is regular, and uses individual skills or competency frameworks as the basis for assessing employees
Appraisal shares the responsibility for results between employee and manager, and requires joint actions to improve results	○ ○ ○ ○ ○ ○	Appraisal is an assessment of the employee by the manager, is a one-way process and is always formally recorded

Source: Extract of sample questions from Magus Indexer culture analysis software

Note: The software used with this culture questionnaire enables (for example) the behaviours of managers in particular areas to be assessed by weighting the responses to combinations of questions against common manager behaviours such as risk averse, excessive involvement in detailed operations, denial of mistakes, etc.

Figure 3.1 Example of indirect questions in a culture questionnaire

their estimates progressively rose to 55 per cent compliance. By this stage, IT staff had 'woken up' to the idea that day-to-day behaviours were important, with a whole range of morale and other quarterly staff engagement indicators showing major step-positive changes as a result (see Chapter 6: Managing your business using informal employee networks).

VIEWS AND CLUES

While not brand-new – independent consultants and researchers at IBM have been mapping informal networks for a number of years – the use of social network analysis as a management tool is accelerating. Given the current emphasis on managing talent, companies are hungry for ways to find and nurture their organizations' most in-the-know employees. And as innovation becomes more critical to corporate survival, the tool lets managers survey the informal interactions between different groups of employees that lead to exciting new ideas. Such a bird's-eye view also exposes the glaring gaps where groups aren't interacting but should be. 'Making the collaboration visible makes it much easier to talk about,' says Kate Ehrlich, a researcher at IBM who studies collaboration.

Source: *The office chart that really counts,* BusinessWeek, February 27 2006

So it's unfortunate, at a time when the ability to create value increasingly depends on the ideas and intangibles of talented workers, that corporate leaders don't do far more to harness the power of informal networks. Valuable as they are, these ad hoc communities clearly have shortcomings: they can increase complexity and confusion, and since they typically fly under management's radar, they elude control.

Source: *Harnessing the power of informal employee networks, The McKinsey Quarterly 2007, Number 4*

'Today, people use the web much more for two-way communication, rather than simply as a medium for receiving information,' says Graham Wylie, head of marketing at Reed Managed Services, part of HR consultancy Reed Consulting.

'In the era of Web 2.0, individuals are disseminating huge amounts of information over the internet through websites, blogs, forums, chatrooms and networking sites. These tools enable groups to quickly and easily keep in contact with each other.'

Wylie says HR must understand that Generation Y – those under the age of 30 – is used to instant messaging and responses. He says HR departments must ensure they are meeting the expectations of employees used to communicating as equals in this way. Only by joining in with corporate social networking can HR take ownership of how its brand is communicated through these channels.

Source: *Getting oomph online: corporate social networking, Personneltoday.com,* 17 September 2007

By this point in the book, readers will not be surprised that key influencers are an important element in overcoming the traditional weaknesses of questionnaire based methods – in particular as applied to ONA exercises. However, the most effective ONA methods typically include four main elements to minimize the impact of survey inaccuracies:

- Support for the ONA exercise and its objectives from relevant senior managers – for example, the CEO, site director, functional director or combinations of these senior executives.

- Interviews with relevant managers, influencers and staff to establish all relevant information before detailed ONA deliverables and full questionnaire design work is carried out. A cross-section of relevant employees is used to test and refine the necessary questionnaires. (Likely outcomes and 'next step' actions are often considered at this stage to ensure that all likely outcomes have been included in the relevant designs, so avoiding or minimizing subsequent follow up ONA surveys.)

- The use of indirect ONA questions (and anonymity options) to maximize accuracy and minimize inaccuracies from respondents who are unwilling to honestly answer sensitive questions, particularly those relating to named colleagues or superiors. These indirect questions can be quite sophisticated with answers to particular questions being 'weighted' so that an overall indication can be derived mathematically from the answers to numerous questions, rather from just one or two (see extract from Magus Indexer questionnaire, Figure 3.1). Where questions are sensitive and specific to named individuals, it may be necessary to identify problems or problem individuals by default – for example, by asking who provides value-added to a particular process, rather than by asking who does not.

- Treating all ONA outputs as inputs into assessment and interpretation workshops (typically made up of relevant managers and key influencers) where underlying as well as obvious issues can be discussed and next step actions agreed.

Analyzing informal personal networks

Early attempts at measuring informal networks relied on relatively crude instruments, such as analyses of e-mail records and simple 'who do you communicate with' questionnaires. Nevertheless, the patterns in simple informal communication networks can often provide a good starting point in determining what is really going on in the workplace.

For example, some key 'central' individuals have very large numbers of informal communication links to colleagues in their workplace (see Figure 3.2) and represent key components of a particular group's set of informal personal networks. Other highly connected individuals perform a different but equally essential role by acting as information 'brokers' between groups (with many informal links coming through them to and from other groups of colleagues). Generally these central individuals and brokers are very accessible communicators who become indispensable to the overall performance of the group. Sometimes, however, they are overworked and stressed – becoming bottlenecks as colleagues increasing rely on them for job-related advice and information. In contrast, individuals with very few communication links may indicate isolation from the workgroup, for example caused by specialization or under-performance. As a rule of thumb, senior managers (and to a lesser extent middle managers) have relatively few informal personal networks – mainly linked to their boss and direct reports.

When analyzing any particular set of informal personal networks, it is important to bear in mind that the configuration of these networks is an evolutionary process, heavily dependent on work situations and individual discretionary actions. Except where regular ONA exercises have been carried out and remedial actions taken, informal personal networks within organizations are almost always very suboptimal in their design and overall impact. Given sufficient time in a stable environment, in theory, it is likely that informal 'evolution' would steadily optimize the design of informal networks. In reality, however, key individuals leave the organization, organizational units are restructured, processes are redesigned and new systems implemented. Sometimes these changes improve the efficiency of informal networks (by chance) but more often the impact of formal changes disrupts the operation of informal personal networks. Put simply, managers and change specialists usually operate in the dark as far as informal networks are concerned. This is yet another reason why business change is a real lottery (with the odds stacked against change sponsors) unless key influencer engagement and informal personal networks form key parts of the change process. (A range of practical uses of ONA is shown in Figure 3.3.)

Managing your business using informal employee networks

Only by using these modern techniques alongside traditional programme and project management, can informal personal network designs be improved to complement the designs for formal changes. (These enhancements of traditional programme and project management are described in Chapter 6: Managing your business using informal employee networks.)

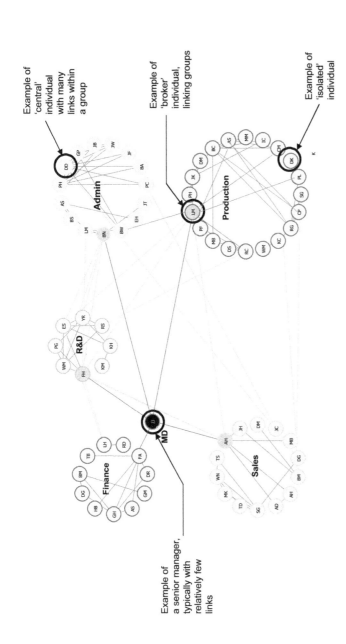

Example of 'central' individual with many links within a group

Example of 'broker' individual, linking groups

Example of 'isolated' individual

Example of a senior manager, typically with relatively few links

Note: This type of informal network diagram can be produced by a wide variety of organizational 'scans', ranging from the identification of key influencers, through communication, knowledge and data sources and value-added patterns, to problem identification and analysis. Changes in specific analysis patterns over time can indicate the success or otherwise of interventions/remedial actions.

Software used: Magus Networker

Figure 3.2   Typical patterns within informal networks

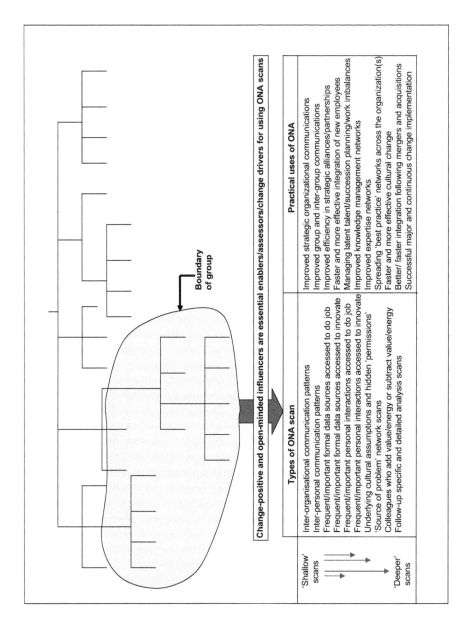

Change-positive and open-minded influencers are essential enablers/assessors/change drivers for using ONA scans

Types of ONA scan	Practical uses of ONA
Inter-organisational communication patterns	Improved strategic organizational communications
Inter-personal communication patterns	Improved group and inter-group communications
Frequent/important formal data sources accessed to do job	Improved efficiency in strategic alliances/partnerships
Frequent/important formal data sources accessed to innovate	Faster and more effective integration of new employees
Frequent/important personal interactions accessed to do job	Managing latent talent/succession planning/work imbalances
Frequent/important personal interactions accessed to innovate	Improved knowledge management networks
Underlying cultural assumptions and hidden 'permissions'	Improved expertise networks
'Source of problem' network scans	Spreading 'best practice' networks across the organization(s)
Colleagues who add value/energy or subtract value/energy	Faster and more effective cultural change
Follow-up specific and detailed analysis scans	Better/ faster integration following mergers and acquisitions
	Successful major and continuous change implementation

Boundary of group

'Shallow' scans

'Deeper' scans

Figure 3.3   Practical uses of Organizational Network Analysis (ONA)

As the use of ONA has matured, more extensive and sophisticated (often) web-based systems have become available that can be tailored to the needs of individual groups or organizations (including indirect questioning to extract sensitive information – for example on which colleagues or groups subtract rather than add value to specific innovation processes).

Modern ONA applications can be viewed as a multi-layered series of informal organizational scans Each scan can be carried out by choosing the appropriate mix of questions for an electronic questionnaire, the results of which are then analyzed through graphic database software and displayed in network form. Those filling in the questionnaire are chosen from appropriate groups across the organization, with relevant change-positive and open-minded influencers both providing guidance during the process and completing the questionnaire themselves – to provide a 'reality check' on the quality and implications of the results. Often the questionnaire exercises need to be expanded, since it is very difficult to predict in advance where all 'invisible' personal networks will extend to when deciding on likely group boundaries.

As well as gathering information on various person-to-person patterns, similar questionnaire techniques can be used for 'person to important data sources' analysis. A multi-layered series of informal organizational scans can therefore be illustrated as a spectrum of shallow through to deep scans, with judgement being needed to decide on the likely value added in progressing to each level of depth, as shown opposite.

Initial interviews with relevant managers and employees are used to establish the boundaries of the group for which the ONA analysis is being carried out, together with the objectives, outputs and scope of the exercise. The most obvious initial ONA scan might be to do a 'health check' on current workplace personal networks across one or more selected business or inter-organizational areas. This initial health check may be as shallow or as deep as you need and can be tailored to address both known and suspected problems and issues. For example:

- Informal interorganizational and interpersonal communication patterns might be analyzed to identify problems with lack of coordination between relevant groups, overworked individuals who are causing roadblocks and delaying the work of others, isolated individuals who are under-performing or key individuals who are limiting access to their unique skills. Often, these analyses make significant use of frequency and value added/ importance questions that can then be subanalyzed by individuals and groups as necessary to provide insights into where key informal communications are taking place and where there may be causes for concern. These insights can be further refined by comparing the results of carefully worded 'are currently happening' questions with the results of relevant 'should be happening' questions.

- Relevant data and knowledge access patterns relating to individuals and groups doing their routine jobs, as well as access patterns when they are innovating or in project mode. Once again, frequency and importance questions are often used to create patterns across individuals, groups and data sources. These patterns can be used to highlight data sources that are not valued or are not being used for various different reasons. Equally, the results will often highlight individuals and groups who are not using data sources that would be valuable to them.

- 'Source of problem' informal network scans can be specially designed to provide insights into suspected problems or issues of concern. This type of ONA scan is usually made up of a multi-stage software questionnaire. First a list of potential problems is scored for frequency/ importance, then potential sources for the top problems are selected in stages – for example, if the problem is categorized as being lack of speedy response by colleagues, the software will then provide groups or even individuals to choose from in order to identify the source of the problem! This type of progressive ONA analysis benefits greatly from early testing by relevant influencers who provide trusted, honest inputs into the design and analysis options that are incorporated.

- 'Energy adding' and 'energy sapping' individuals can also be identified through carefully designed ONA scans (see Figure 3.4). Once again, a multi-stage software questionnaire is often used. The first stage is typically to select the business activity or type of initiative for which you want (in the second stage) to identify those colleagues who 'add energy' or 'subtract energy' from the process.

- Underlying cultural assumptions and hidden permissions (the unwritten rules about 'how we really do things here') can also be clarified through appropriately designed ONA scans. For example, by combining indirect questions and analysis weightings with information about the participants (business area, job level in organization), differences in the cultural perceptions in different parts and different levels of the organization can be highlighted. Frequently, the perceptions of senior managers differ in some areas from those of middle managers, with coal face employees experiencing a very different working world from that envisioned by senior executives.

- Any or all of the techniques described above can be tailored into specific single or multi-level ONA scans to analyze specific business environments and their associated informal personal networks.

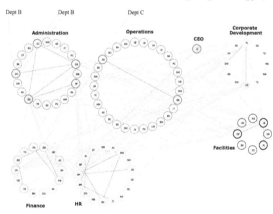

Figure 3.4   'High energy' people are prominent in informal communication networks

Sometimes the results of one particular ONA scan will raise unforeseen issues that require further ONA follow-up scans. Early use of relevant, usually local, trusted key influencers in the design and testing stages can minimize the number for follow-up scans.

With a technique as powerful and all-embracing as ONA, care and some skill are needed to ensure that the work focuses on the practical value-adding

---

VIEWS AND CLUES

We found a critical link between a person's position in the (energy) network and his or her performance as measured by annual human resource ratings. In all surveys, we assessed information flow in the entire network as well as each person's use of impersonal sources such as files and databases. We anticipated that those who tapped their informational environment more effectively would be better performers. Intriguingly, we found in all three settings that performance was closely connected to people's positions in the energy network. Even after accounting for the use of various personal and impersonal sources of information, we found that those who energized others were much higher performers.

Source: *The Hidden Powers of Social Networks*, Rob Cross & Andrew Parker, Harvard Business School Press, 2004, p. 54

Professional women are building careers and tackling workplace inequality through all-female networking groups. According to the think tank Demos, 'new girl networks' are challenging the power of the informal 'old boy network'.

Its report, Girlfriends in High Places, points to a growth in women's professional networks.

It looks at how men use informal networks to get ahead, particularly in hierarchical establishments. In the Civil Service, women account for 26 per cent of senior posts, and now have their own network for female civil servants.

Source: *Women-only networks set up to boost promotion prospects, Personneltoday.com*, 27 April 2004

Each week a million searches are conducted on IBM's Blue Pages, a corporate social network set up long before MySpace or Facebook became popular. The aim was to connect employees and contractors, to help sales people with leads, and to ensure that everyone felt part of a cohesive team.

Ethan McCarthy is editor-in-chief of IBM's Intranet. 'Blue Pages is an essential part of IBM,' he says. 'Each employee has his own page which is full of information. It enables managers to find workers with the skills and experience they require, which makes building teams easier.'

Rather than banning Facebook and MySpace, some employers have decided that it could be better to compete with them and provide an alternative.

Source: *Need a team? Get on the network, The Times*, 2 April 2008

elements and does not become just an academic exercise, swamped by 100 per cent samples and the resulting multiple, over-complicated network diagrams that are impossible to interpret. Careful questionnaire design and selecting 'optimum' samples of questionnaire responders are crucial to the success of ONA. In doing this, local managers working with selected local influencers are far more effective than senior executives or external consultants (who should provide guidance on the process, not determine the content).

After all, extensive collaboration across *all* departments in an organization might seem a worthy objective in theory but in practice there is a very real danger of overkill. People have a limited amount of time to develop and maintain informal relationships. Just as organizations learnt to refine and redesign their formal processes, so they will need to learn how to focus their efforts on developing and maintaining essential value-adding informal personal networks. Certainly, blind acceptance of raw ONA data would often be foolish. Many of the central people in an informal communications network are secretaries and general administrative managers, who are generally *not* important elements in the value adding business process. Equally, a lot of the 'traffic' through informal networks is gossip, jokes and personal information – so take care before investing in any automated network analysis tools that seek to eliminate human intervention and judgement.

Take care when 'formalizing the informal'

When using influencer engagement techniques and ONA to enhance the effectiveness of informal personal networks for business purposes, there is only one overriding golden rule:

> *'Never forget that you are dealing with informal personal networks, where individuals ultimately decide what they personally will agree to do.'*

Informal personal networks are an important safety valve for discontent, as well as a powerful mechanism for enhancing business and organizational performance. Wise executives will recognize that it will never be possible to fully optimize informal personal networks from a business point of view. They will ensure that both the culture and the mechanisms available to improve informal network effectiveness are in place and strongly supported across the formal organization. But they will never attempt to force changes in their informal 'shadow' organizations by management decree. Formal decrees regarding informal personal networks are a recipe for rapid negative communication across all informal networks – for widespread employee disillusion, and for a truly dysfunctional organization.

In any case, using ONA to make otherwise-hidden informal networks visible, so that they can be formalized and controlled, is self-defeating. As soon as formal networks are set up by management, new informal networks will evolve, and these will be just as hidden and mysterious as those that management tried to control. This is yet another misplaced application of old, tired command and control management.

Changing and creating new informal personal networks

Once you have carried out carefully considered and well-designed ONA exercises and held all the relevant follow up 'assessment and interpretation' workshops, you will have a clear understanding of current informal network problems and constraints. At this point in the process, it is relatively easy to identify the changes that would (ideally) improve the overall business effectiveness of relevant personal networks across key areas of your organization and into key external stakeholders. Once again, relevant local influencers will be able to put these ideas to the 'real world' test and suggest what is achievable and when.

A raft of different techniques are available to wise managers as they seek to often enhance, sometimes restrain and fundamentally improve their informal networks. Wisdom comes in the choices made on when and how these techniques are put into practice:

- Change the physical location of *relevant* employees to increase opportunities for informal contact. In some cases this might tip the balance on site locations in favour of fewer somewhat larger sites. (For example, Chrysler brought all their people involved in new car development back into one location.) On others, it might simply mean relocating relevant staff from different groups onto the same open-plan floor or redesigning communal areas and communal services.

  Build collaboration and knowledge sharing as key behaviours into performance management systems. (Where these systems promote individualistic behaviour, an unexpected consequence is often that informal networks are relatively thin on the ground and disconnected.) Where relevant, this should include cross-organization collaboration.

- Hold cross-organizational training events, workshops and social events to help build social ties between people in *relevant*, different parts of the organization. 'Knowledge fairs' are an interesting innovation where each relevant part of the organization sets up a stall at the fair to promote its particular set of skills and knowledge to visitors from other organizational areas.

- Use specific rewards, such as bonuses, special meals or store credits to celebrate individuals who make the special effort to help colleagues. Rather like performance management systems, these rewards will only be effective if they are seen a genuine and reflect reality. The day when a management 'favourite' who is known to be less than accessible gets promoted or receives a public reward for collaborative behaviour is the day when these incentives become meaningless to an increasingly cynical workforce!

- Use a recruitment and promotion process – often a group problem-solving exercise – that strongly selects individuals who exhibit collaborative behaviours.

- Set up staff rotation and cross-area mentoring initiatives to inform key individuals about the skills and knowledge available in other groups, as well as to 'seed' potential future informal personal networks. (Remember, some will fall on stony ground, and some will require several informal meetings – through different mechanisms - to flourish, so don't be tempted to force the natural pace.)

- Put selected individuals, particularly new staff, onto internal or external projects together with experienced colleagues with extensive personal networks. Not only is this likely to move a relatively isolated person closer to extensive informal communications, it also encourages further links indirectly through the heavily-connected individuals in the project team.

- Remove some areas of responsibility from overworked central or broker individuals, while encouraging those taking on the extra responsibility to extend their own personal networks to include new contacts that are relevant to the added role. Alternatively, train and mentor these key highly-connected individuals to manage their time better and/or hand off some of their advisory roles to other capable colleagues.

- Use appropriate technology to increase awareness of expertise across the organization through skill profiling systems, knowledge sharing through knowledge management systems, and other relevant technology-based tools.

VIEWS AND CLUES

In one high-tech company we worked with, several of the leading researchers were threatening to resign. Senior management was blind-sided by this news because the team had been extremely successful at developing new technologies and introducing them to the rest of the company, and their work had been handsomely rewarded and recognised. But a social network analysis showed that the organisation was destroying the group because it did not recognise that most of the scientists were peripheral specialists. As the researchers came up with winning applications, senior managers started asking them to attend more internal meetings and to present their findings to large customers.

Because of their successes, the demands on the researchers' time increased so much that they felt unable to stay at the cutting edge of their expertise, let alone advance it. Management did not recognise that these researchers needed to maintain their peripheral position for their own satisfaction and career success.

Source: *The Hidden Powers of Social Networks*, Rob Cross & Andrew Parker, Harvard Business School Press, 2004, pp. 80–81

Promoting someone to the role of manager is a curious activity. You move someone who is good at their job into a role requiring completely different skills which they may not possess. And you pay them more.

Despite the rise of the 'professional manager', such moves are still common. They are one of the few ways of preventing valued staff from looking elsewhere for better pay and prospects.

Yet seasoned managers can easily forget just how difficult many people find the transition from peer to manager. The people who used to huddle around the coffee machine with you putting the corporate world to rights don't seem quite so eager to open up any more. Should you still go down the pub with them, or would it be an invasion of their space? If you don't, will they just think you're stuck up?

For the new manager, this enforced change of identity is a major challenge. Neil Jones, now head of HR development at the Welsh Development Agency, remembers finding himself in this position when he was working in local government. He says three things changed when he was promoted.

'The first was the perception of my boss. Suddenly I was a manager, and his expectations of me were different. The second thing was the perception of the people below me – they had to look at me in a different way, but weren't sure what the ground rules would be in terms of their relationship with me.'

'The third shift was in my perception of myself. I think that's often the most difficult and lonely shift to manage. You are caught between the great divide with one foot in the management camp and the other wanting to be with your former peers.'

Source: *In at the deep end*, Personneltoday.com, 10 October 2000

- Carry out regular, relevant ONA exercises to measure the changes that result from your chosen combination of the above techniques. Evaluate what has been achieved, learn the lessons through dialogue and move forward to encourage further improvements in network optimization linked to your business strategy. Learn when to pause in the process, but never let there be any doubt that this is an ongoing priority approach, based on collaboration and mutual consent, that will never 'go away'.

Needless to say, as managers go through the process of encouraging personal informal networks to migrate towards a near optimal design, the relevant key influencers – those change-positive and open-minded people again – will have a major role to play in advising on the right actions, as well as creating an environment where these sorties into the shadow organization are understood and widely accepted.

Chapter summary

Business change programmes in recent years have led to organizations with fewer levels of hierarchy and more flexible organizational boundaries. Organizational silos have been targeted again and again as major constraints to business efficiency and effectiveness. A by-product of these structural changes is that much effective work increasingly occurs through informal networks of interpersonal relationships, rather than through formal reporting structures or work processes. As a consequence, these invisible networks have become fundamental to performance and strategy execution.

ONA provides a pictorial scan of the informal organizational activities. It is a powerful means of making invisible patterns of informal communications flow, knowledge access and collaboration visible.

However, when questionnaires are used in work environments, inaccuracies can become very serious and even undermine the whole validity of the exercise. The reasons can be summarized under two main headings - fear and lethargy. To overcome these problems, the most effective ONA methods typically include four main elements to minimize the impact of survey inaccuracies:

- Support for the ONA exercise and its objectives from relevant senior managers.

- Interviews with relevant managers, influencers and staff to establish all relevant information before detailed ONA deliverables and full questionnaire design work are carried out.

- The use of indirect ONA questions (and anonymity options) to maximize accuracy and minimize inaccuracies from respondents who are unwilling to honestly answer sensitive questions.

- Treating all ONA outputs as inputs into assessment and interpretation workshops (typically made up of relevant managers and key influencers) where underlying as well as obvious issues can be discussed and next step actions agreed.

VIEWS AND CLUES

In summarising a decade's worth of studies, Tom Allen of MIT indicated that engineers and scientists were roughly five times as likely to turn to a person for information as to an impersonal source such as a database or a file cabinet. In other settings, research has consistently shown that whom you know has a significant impact on what you come to know, because relationships are critical for obtaining information, solving problems, and learning how to do your work.

On reflection, this is not very surprising, but in our work we wanted to reconfirm this point given the recent explosion of information and technology. Each time we conducted a network assessment, we also surveyed employees about their use of available technologies. Only once did we find an organisation where employees rated internal databases or knowledge management systems as more effective than the internet in helping them complete their work. In no cases did we see any technology come close to the importance people gave to other people for finding information and learning how to get work done.

Source: *The Hidden Powers of Social Networks,* Rob Cross & Andrew Parker, Harvard Business School Press, 2004, p. 11

One of the truisms of communications is that nothing travels faster than the speed of rumor. We express constant amazement that information moves through our company, usually distorted as it passes from one person to another. We deride gossips and urge people not to take part in watercooler discussions. Home offices issue a constant stream of memos aimed at quelling rumors. Yet, rumors persist, oftentimes overwhelming the official communications. Worse, the so-called rumor mill often contains more accurate information than the official channels. People seem to ferret out the truth, regardless of whether we know it ourselves.

Source: *Harness the power of the informal communications network, TechRepublic,* 30 October 2003

A raft of different techniques are available to wise managers as they seek to enhance, restrain and fundamentally improve their informal networks. Wisdom comes in the choices made on when and how these techniques are put into practice.

When using influencer engagement techniques and ONA to enhance the effectiveness of informal personal networks for business purposes, there is only one overriding golden rule:

'Never forget that you are dealing with informal *personal* networks, where *individuals* ultimately decide what they *personally* will agree to do.'

VIEWS AND CLUES

You always know when you are in a Hot Spot. You feel energized and vibrantly alive. Your brain is buzzing with ideas, and the people around you share your joy and excitement. The energy is palpable, bright, shining. These are times when what you and others have always known becomes clearer, when adding value becomes more possible. Times when the ideas and insights from others miraculously combine with your own in a process of synthesis from which spring novelty, new ideas, and innovation. Times when you explore together what previously seemed opaque and distant. We can all remember being in Hot Spots, when working with other people was never more exciting and exhilarating and when you knew deep in your heart that what you were jointly achieving was important and purposeful. On such occasions, time seems to rush by as you and those around you are 'in the flow'. Time even seems to stand still. We enjoy being part of a Hot Spot, and we are healthier, happier people as a result.

When Hot Spots arise in and between companies, they provide energy for exploiting and applying knowledge that is already known and genuinely exploring what was previously unknown. As a consequence, Hot Spots are marvelous creators of value for organizations and wonderful, life-enhancing phenomena for each of us.

Source: 'Hot Spots', Lynda Gratton, FT Prentice Hall, 2007

Individuals vary in the time spent in 'flow'. Over one third of those surveyed in US and German polls (responding to slightly different questions) estimated that they rarely or never experienced involvement so intense that they lose touch of time (42 per cent of Americans, 35 per cent of Germans), whereas about one fifth (16 per cent of Americans, 23 per cent of Germans) reported having such experiences daily.

Source: *Handbook of Positive Psychology*, CR Snyder and Shane J Lopez, Oxford University Press, 2002

Balancing Formal and Informal Employee Networks

Formal organizations – with all their formal roles and responsibilities, business processes, IT systems and command and control history, can be severely inhibited by conflicting informal personal networks and influencer balances.

Similarly, informal 'shadow' organizations – driven as they are by collaboration and personal choice – can be transformed overnight from relatively efficient networks of personal interactions into disconnected demoralized fragments by a few misconceived organizational, process or systems changes. Think – the next time you decide to restructure the organization, how many informal networks will that break up and destroy? You mean you don't know?

Both these scenarios are avoidable given what we now know about informal networks. It's just that the way that we approach business change needs to change – a lot!

Looking back at the lessons learnt from the pioneers who used influencers and informal personal networks to make change happen in their organizations, the single biggest hurdle to overcome was undoubtedly the initial senior managers' mindsets. Once this was overcome, the mechanics were relatively straightforward and the interest shown by those engaged in the process (particularly the influencers) generated an enthusiasm that was very similar to the 'hot spots' of intense work and enjoyment described by Lynda Gratton in her book 'Hot Spots' (see Views and Clues).

Different types of business change

In designing formal and informal processes for identifying and successfully implementing business change, the fundamental types of change are best described by the impact of the proposed change on people. From this perspective, there are three, and only three, distinct types of business change:

1.   'Radical Disruptive' business change, which is radical from a business perspective, and has large impacts on people working in the business in relatively short timescales. Examples of this type of change include cultural alignment following mergers, major business transformation/ re-engineering initiatives and large downsizing exercises, where remaining staff need to take on extra or different work.

2.   'Radical Structural' business change, is radical from a business perspective but has only limited impact on people working in the business. Examples of this type of change typically include company disposals (which often have little impact on the remaining business areas), high-level organizational restructuring, new product introductions through well-established processes, and expansion into new geographic areas with new people.

3.   'Incremental' business change, typified by continuous improvement initiatives, which takes place progressively over time and have a cumulative impact on people. Examples of this type of change include most local quality improvement initiatives, small-scale process and system improvements, moderate changes in reward/ payment criteria and local organizational changes.

While influencers and highly connected individuals can, and often should, be used to good effect in all three types of business change, their potential impact varies considerably in each type of change. They are absolutely fundamental to success in 'Radical Disruptive' business change. They are very important during ongoing 'Incremental' business change. However, they may be needed only occasionally during 'Radical Structural' changes. Despite this, care should be taken to ensure that any changes implemented by management decision alone should not adversely affect trust and goodwill between managers and influencers/highly connected individuals and other employees. (The typical activities of selected influencers and highly connected individuals during a 'Radical Disruptive' business change initiative are outlined below.)

INFLUENCER AND HIGHLY CONNECTED INDIVIDUAL ACTIVITIES DURING 'RADICAL DISRUPTIVE' CHANGE

Over the entire period of a change programme, starting at the point where a draft vision has been prepared, relevant influencers and highly connected individuals will be identified and engaged in a range of change activities, determined by the change sponsor and other relevant senior managers in agreement with the programme director/manager and relevant line managers. These activities typically include:

- reviewing and suggesting practical enhancements/additions to the change vision to make implementation easier or more effective;

- contributing to ongoing 'readiness for change' analysis by providing regular assessments of local colleague support for the changes;

- being members of a communications review group (which meets monthly) – possibly on a rotating basis;

- being user representatives on change teams (systems, process, organizational, rewards and recognition, training, cultural, relocation, and so on);

- preparing and completing informal organizational scan questionnaires;

- attending workshops to discuss issues and identify solutions to the problems highlighted through organizational scans;

- identifying and agreeing practical behaviours to support the organization's agreed values;

- engaging in culture change initiatives to encourage and challenge day-to-day behaviours in line with agreed, desired behaviours;

- providing on-going advice on new actions and organizational mechanisms that would help drive the change programme;

- identifying problem areas where interventions might be needed rapidly to minimize the impact;

- identifying influential, change positive or open-minded colleagues who have the skills necessary to fill new and existing management roles as these become necessary during the change process;

- contributing to local continuous improvement initiatives, where these are in keeping with overall change programme activities and objectives.

Egos and conflicts of interest

The relative roles of managers, influencers and highly connected individuals during business change can be difficult to get right. After all, one of the key principles of traditional management theory is that managers should have both the authority and the responsibility for delivering change within their area. The use of influencers and others, as well as managers, during change has therefore the potential to violate this fundamental principle.

On the other hand, experience tells us that on average fewer than 40 per cent of first line managers and supervisors are respected enough by their subordinates to have a significant impact on their views on change. Indeed, in many organizations, a high percentage of the first line managers/supervisors who influence downwards are not change positive by nature (or in reality). Do you really want to leave the fate of an important business change in local managements' hands because of 'command and control' management theories about authority and responsibility?

Nevertheless, in practice, achieving effective engagement alongside effective ego 'smoothing' is often not as difficult as it seems, providing that manager sensitivities are anticipated and reflected during the change process. There is a long tradition that managers are responsible for formal change communication (with limited direct involvement in change details), while user representatives (at lower levels) often get involved in detailed change design and implementation planning. This tradition can be used to facilitate the extensive use of selected influencers and highly connected individuals across the change process, while still leaving the more formal elements of change initiation and communication to the formal management hierarchy. Where conflicts arise between local managers and local influencers, more senior managers can invoke their powers of persuasion (and occasionally their authority) to drive through the required result (at least at a formal level).

Employee engagement is widely touted as a highly effective way to move towards a 'high performance workplace'. However, few, if any, of the many books and magazine articles on the subject ever address the practical constraints – it's just impractical to have all employees engaged on detailed change ideas and activities, all at once. The most effective approach by far is to have a two-tiered approach:

1.   A broad range of opportunities for all employees to become engaged from time to time – such as effective internal communications and feedback mechanisms, a framework that encourages everyone to contribute ideas for continuous improvement, regular question and answer sessions both locally and with senior managers, and so on.

2.   A focused approach to change initiatives, where selected influencers and highly connected individuals are actively engaged on a

significant (but generally part-time) basis to help design and then implement effective business changes – for all types of business change.

By looking at potential sensitivities for each of the main participants during a change initiative, effective and selective engagement tactics can be employed, as follows:

- Employees *not* identified as being 'influential' or highly connected change agents are generally not surprised that they have not been selected. With the exception of a few ambitious individuals who feel left out plus staff who are broadly change-negative, most staff are generally pleased that some local influencers who many of them respect/trust are being involved in the change. The end result is that more staff are pleased with these arrangements (and open to persuasion) than with traditional manager-dominated change processes.

- Employees identified as being 'influential' or highly connected change agents are flattered and motivated to get involved in change. The end result is that a much larger number of effective local change agents are engaged than with traditional change processes.

- Managers/supervisors identified as being 'influential' change agents are flattered and motivated to get involved in change. The end result is that they are more likely to be active in change due to their 'change credentials' being recognized.

- Change-negative managers/supervisors *not* identified as being 'influential' change agents are concerned and nervous that their 'change blocker' tendencies have been recognized. Their response is an initial knee-jerk opposition to the whole informal network process, followed by much greater reluctance to openly (or even obliquely) oppose change once the change process starts due to perceived 'outing'. They are also more likely to accept an exit option, such as voluntary redundancy, and less likely to apply for promotion/sideways moves into post-change management roles.

- Change-positive and open-minded managers/supervisors not identified as being 'influential' change agents are concerned and nervous that they have not been identified as 'good managers' for the future. Some of these individuals have the capability to develop their influence in future, while others do not (and mostly represent failures in past selection/promotion processes). The end result is that these individuals are less likely to be active in the change process. They will need lots of support by senior managers and change practitioners before and during change transition. One rule of thumb is to engage them as much as possible in local, formal change communications and discussions.

By being sensitive and adopting suitable tactics when dealing with each of the above type of stakeholders during a change process, experience shows that many of the early fears about bruised egos and disappointments can readily be overcome. Indeed, the process tends to rapidly highlight issues that would need to be addressed anyway.

VIEWS AND CLUES

Why do people indulge in negative behaviour? We know that effective management behaviour is determined by the requirements of the job, and therefore as job requirements change we must modify our behaviour appropriately to meet them. However, negative behaviour is not required by any job. So why does it happen? Is it just a quirk of human nature – or are there other reasons?

The first thing to understand is that performance blocking behaviour is situation rather than personality driven. Because personality is fixed at about age three (see The Journal of Personality, *August 2003), if performance blocking behaviour were a manifestation of personality an individual would show the same type of behaviour regardless of the situation. However we find that people often display negative behaviour at work that they don't use outside the work environment. It is learned behaviour, and* *fortunately what is learned can be unlearned*

Source: *Performance Blocking Behaviour 1,* Dr R Stuart-Kotze, Behaviourkinetics.com

Larry ran our dispensable-rotating-objects division in the Midwest. We acquired it a few years ago, and with it came Larry, its chief executive. From the start he didn't know what it meant to work as a team. You could feel his bad vibrations all the way from Minneapolis on a conference call. He never volunteered information. His people were secretive. His numbers stank.

It's been clear for several years that Larry was a tumor on the body of the enterprise. And yet he stayed on, and on, and on, until finally his act got just too old, and wham! now he's out of here. I think he was permitted to gunk things up for so long for two reasons: (1) Nobody had a better idea of what to do with his job, and (2) It's really hard to fire another manager face-to-face.

Source: *A tale of three firings*, Fortune, 13 July 2007

Perhaps the most sensitive of these are situations where specific individuals (often middle managers and sometimes senior managers) have been identified as potential change blockers because of their past behaviours. Despite a natural tendency on the part of many change sponsors and some change professionals to 'lance the boil' and sort out the problem early (typically through dismissal, redundancy or a transfer out of the relevant business area), experience shows that such radical action is only effective in extreme cases. In most situations, forcing out a potential change blocker, particularly a person who is a reasonably popular local change-negative influencer, can lead to a 'martyrdom' effect: 'Look how unfairly they treated poor old John – he may have been a moaner but he did not deserve this!' Where strong action is taken in this way, disillusion can easily set in, diminishing both the motivation and effectiveness of local change-positive influencers and well-connected individuals.

Some early change management practice suggested that a special effort should be made to 'bring potential change blockers on board'. The logic behind this approach is that by converting influential change-negative individuals, the result was sometimes very positive – 'there is no one more enthusiastic than a convert'. However, experience shows that the convert ratio is typically small and that the effort needed is disproportionate, particularly during high pressure, limited resource change programmes.

In practice, a balanced approach is generally the most effective in dealing with potential change blockers. This approach is sometimes called 'the clean sheet' approach. In effect, a key part of change communications is to stress to all affected employees – often informally – that past change-negative behaviour is wiped clean: all employees will be treated fairly and assessed on their behaviours from now on. This does not mean that potential change blockers will be chosen to participate in change activities or as part of change teams. Generally, they will not. The psychology here is very interesting. Change-negative individuals usually 'know' or strongly suspect that they have been identified as potential blockers by their colleagues. Their typical response, after an initial burst of resistance against the informal network process, is to 'lie low' and avoid being viewed as a problem. A few previously change-negative individuals, however, will respond by becoming very proactive and volunteer to work on change teams. The 'clean sheet' approach recommends that a limited number of such individuals should be included in change teams, provided always that the balance of numbers/opinions in each team remains strongly change-positive. After all, having a sceptic around can sometimes add a useful reality check, providing that the person does not become disruptive to team effectiveness.

As mentioned earlier, by adopting an informal network approach alongside more formal programme and project management techniques, change initiatives will benefit from a much more coordinated and effective informal environment compared to traditional methods. By using Organizational Network Analysis (ONA) scans, change programmes can create quite efficient informal network designs operating in favour of change, compared to the largely fragmented and uncoordinated informal environment where potential change blockers are operating. In effect, most potential blockers will have only 'second-hand' information from the formal change programme (by and large, they are not on change teams) and they will be operating in the dark about most informal personal networks. There really is no need to create martyrs during successful change initiatives.

(Remember that informal networks form spontaneously and are volatile, so designed networks always break down to some degree. With a good network of enabled influencers, there will be a hidden, guiding non-management hand at work facilitating the volatile emergence of efficient and effective networks, even though these will evolve and change over time.)

Bounded freedom

When relevant senior managers sit down to consider the particular influencers and highly connected individuals to be engaged in business change or product/ service innovation, they are themselves being engaged in the change process. This selection process applies a level of management judgement to the raw influencer and informal personal network analyses, builds management support for the process and sets out a framework for empowering the chosen individuals.

This empowerment exercise typically takes the form of a 'Bounded Freedom' framework (see Figure 4.1), where line managers exercise formal control in day-to-day work but the selected influencers have considerable freedom to participate innovatively in relevant change activities. Specifically, this freedom includes the explicit permission to influencers and highly connected individuals to report bad news to management, as well as good, without fear or favour. Typical guidelines for creating the 'Bounded Freedom' within which both managers and selected influencers/connected individuals can operate effectively include the following key elements:

- Line managers continue to have full authority across all relevant day-to-day work activities. They will continue to authorize any

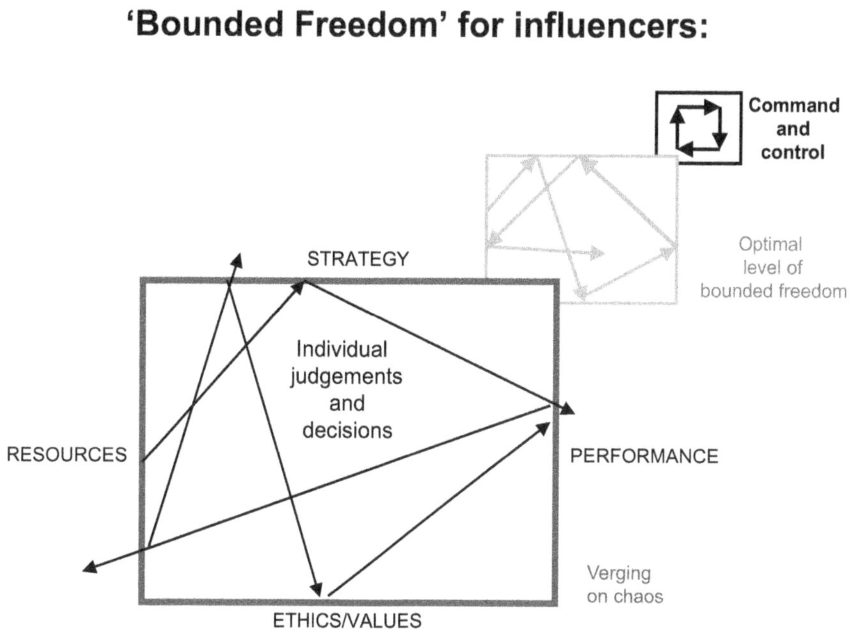

'Bounded Freedom' for influencers:

Figure 4.1   **Illustrating the concept of 'Bounded Freedom'**

employee secondments and absences due to work on change initiatives.

- Relevant senior managers/change sponsors will communicate both formally and informally with all engaged influencers/connected individuals in an open and honest way, treating them as intelligent adults and often trusting them with sensitive information ahead of formal announcements.

- Selected influencers and highly connected individuals will be free to express their views and ideas, free to communicate informally with their colleagues, and free to communicate informally on change issues with senior managers.

- All change ideas will be assessed on their merits, not on who made the suggestion.

Balancing formal and informal employee networks in operational improvement

During day-to-day operational activities, formal employee networks (as broadly indicated in organizational charts, business process/systems procedures, HR

VIEWS AND CLUES

I was asked to write an article exposing the problems with performance appraisal for a Sunday Newspaper. I submitted my first draft and the editor suggested I should provide balance by talking about what to do instead. My response was that you don't need to find an alternative to doing a bad thing – you should just stop it. He said: 'Ring your friends in Japan and find out what they do'. So I did. I asked: 'What do you do about performance appraisal?' The reply was: 'What is that?' I explained. Japanese people tend to be too polite to laugh. In Toyota the HR strategy places emphasis on management's responsibilities. For example, there are no less than 44 questions the manager must address to ensure the employees work in a system that enables them to perform.

Another way to put it is to ask: 'What are all the questions I should address as a leader before I decide I have a "people problem"?' Asking these questions of your system helps you discover how few people problems you have and how much responsibility for performance rests on you – the leader.

Source: John Seddon, Freedom from Command and Control, Vanguard Press, 2003, p. 123

What happens when bad measures drive out good is strikingly described in an article in the current Economic Journal. Investigating the effects of competition in the NHS, Carol Propper and her colleagues made an extraordinary discovery. Under competition, hospitals improved their patient waiting times. At the same time, the death rate following emergency heart attack admissions substantially increased. Why? As targets, waiting times were and are measured (and what gets measured gets managed, right?). Emergency heart attack deaths were not tracked and therefore not managed. Even though no one would argue that the trade-off – shorter waiting times but more deaths – was anything but a travesty of NHS purpose, that's what the choice of measure produced.

Source: The rule is simple: be careful what you measure, The Observer, 10 February 2008

policies, and so on) are viewed as dominant. This is the environment in which most traditional first line managers feel comfortable and in control. Nevertheless, even here, informal networks – in the form of influencers (of all types) and highly connected individuals – typically dominate the local culture and the local informal communications network. They also dominate in situations where problems and issues arise that need to be resolved, and they should play a significant role in continuous improvement activities, particularly where cross-area collaboration is needed. Given our understanding of the importance of balancing formal and informal networks, it is interesting to consider how closely the really successful continuous improvement experiences mirror or diverge from the influencer/highly connected individual engagement approach.

In looking at really successful continuous improvement programmes that have delivered huge benefits over many years, there is probably only one obvious candidate against which to cross-check any new informal network approach to continuous improvement – Toyota.

- So, is Toyota using informal networks to drive their prodigious continuous improvement success? At first glance, the most obvious answer is 'not yet'. But digging deeper, there are strong clues that indicate that many of the prerequisites for informal network success are already in place. Far from being a rigid command and control organization, Toyota has consistently used the following approaches that will be familiar by now to readers of this book. They use behaviour and problem-solving exercises when recruiting new employees. Collaborative behaviours (including the ability to work well in teams) are key selection criteria. This applies particularly to the selection and promotion of managers at all levels. (See Chapter 5: Throwing out those tired old HR models.) The Toyota interpretation of 'bounded freedom' is all embracing. At Toyota everyone within the organization, from executive to shop floor worker, is challenged to use their initiative and creativity to experiment and learn.

- Toyota empower their employees to a surprising extent – any production line worker can stop the line if they suspect there is a problem.

- The Toyota business 'system' and team working are the subjects for assessment, not annual assessments of the performance of individual employees.

Continuous improvement is endemic to the company's culture – The Toyota Way – and is taken very seriously, from the top to the bottom of the organization. As a result, Toyota employees generate over one million process improvement ideas annually. The more astonishing number is the fact that 90 per cent of those ideas are implemented.

By analyzing these 'clues' from the informal networks perspective, some tentative conclusions may be drawn as to why Toyota is so successful. First of all, the culture of continuous improvement is stable and rock solid. Although new ideas and initiatives are continually being generated and implemented, the continuous improvement initiative itself never dies or gets suspended by management whim: all employees – managers, staff and operators – know where they stand. All the incentives and the underlying culture (the way we do things here) encourage all staff to be innovative.

So, good, the entire work environment is supportive to change – but what is likely to be going on in the idea generation and change implementation processes? Well, first of all, those employees with extensive informal personal networks are likely to be key contributors to the process. They will have access to a larger idea pool through their contacts plus a greater understanding of the environment outside their work group when compared to more isolated colleagues. They will also have a larger natural population whom they can draw on to discuss and refine ideas, suggesting that a high percentage of their ideas are likely to be accepted and implemented. Even if these key individuals are not particularly good at thinking up new ideas themselves, they are ideally placed to act as very efficient catalysts in developing and communicating the ideas of others. Many, but not all, of the highly connected people will also be influencers, with the capability of enthusing others about relevant ideas and so speeding up the innovative process. But equally important, they are likely to have a number of strong influencers amongst their contacts, who can bring even more influencing 'muscle' to the process. Where influencers or highly connected individuals are also 'brokers' who influence and connect outside their immediate work areas, their impact on innovation is spread even wider, with a wider range of inputs and greater influencing potential.

So, is the overall informal network design that has evolved at Toyota likely to be very efficient for continuous innovation? Well, because of the stable 'continuous improvement' environment that has been in place in established sites for many years, the overall designs there have probably evolved quite well. In newer locations, these efficiencies may be somewhat diluted, despite the 'follow best practice' mechanisms that Toyota has in place. Overall though, there is likely to be a significant opportunity for improvement in informal network designs. Prediction: even Toyota will become more effective at continuous improvement once they adopt informal networks as an important part of their continuous change toolkit.

Balancing formal and informal employee networks during major change

Until the late 1990s, programme and project management methods (see Figure 4.2 overview) were very weak at addressing the human aspects of change. With luck, a change professional working on a big change programme in the early 1990s would have a primitive guide to stakeholder analysis and some rough

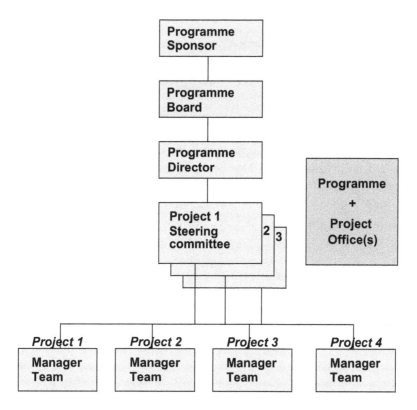

Figure 4.2   Traditional programme and project management

rules regarding user involvement to play with. Today the same person would not only have accurately identified key influencers and highly connected individuals to work with, but would also have clear guidelines in how to use these key players alongside managers during the change process. These advances have given change professionals two major advantages over their early 1990s counterparts – an effective implementation mechanism through the power of influencers and the ability to significantly improve informal personal networks to enhance the effectiveness of all their other formal networks of processes, systems, and so on. Where in the early 1990s the change professional would have about a 30 per cent chance of achieving most of the business objectives of change, the equivalent change professional today can confidently expect at be close to a 90 per cent success rate when measured across all the main business change objectives. (The only significant exceptions to this rule are where the change involves major risks due to pioneering fundamentally new IT 'solutions'. In practice, these are surprisingly rare events since most IT change failures are due to 'people factors', rather than real technological difficulties.)

THE NATURAL LAYERS OF INTEGRATED FORMAL/INFORMAL CHANGE

The integrated use of influencer engagement techniques and ONA is comprehensive, covering all aspects of the people side of change. It can be designed and tailored to meet the requirements of any major or continuous improvement change programme. Because these new techniques focus on the people who should be involved in change and the coordination/enhancement of relevant informal personal networks, they are fully compatible with all established project and programme management methods and with all change design and control methods. The use of integrated influencer engagement techniques and ONA can be viewed as a series of concentric layers, see Figure 4.3, starting with a core inner layer that determines the people (managers, influencers and highly connected individuals) who will be most effective in driving through the desired changes, on time and within budget.

The inner layer of this integrated approach focuses on getting the right people in place and facilitating ways that these individuals can work effectively together, with change programme staff and with relevant managers at all levels. The key people behind every successful, ambitious change programme are a group of committed managers, influencers, highly connected individuals and change professionals working together as a team to make change happen. Traditional definitions of change agents are now redundant. Those nominated as change agents in the past have all too often been the wrong people – either ineffective in their impact on colleagues or simply not motivated strongly enough in favour of change. The most effective change agents in any organization are change-positive individuals who strongly influence their colleagues in the work environment. The next most effective group of change agents are those who are strongly influential but are open minded on change. Experience shows

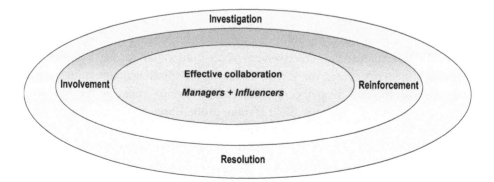

Figure 4.3   Scope of integrated influencer engagement and Organizational Network Analysis (ONA)

that both these groups of 'real' change agents need to be actively engaged at different stages in a change programme if the chances of consistent success are to be high. The inner core (and early stages) of the approach is therefore concerned with:

- Gaining management understanding and support for working with these 'real' change agents (and giving up some traditional practices of 'nominating' staff as change agents). This is facilitated through a series of management workshops, starting with the most senior management team and cascading downwards through the relevant management structure – supported by a relevant senior manager at each step. The main elements in this integrated informal networks approach are presented and discussed, with particular focus on the roles of managers and influencers in the change process. Key individuals in change programme management roles must also be included in this process at an early stage.

- Accurately identifying the change-positive and open-minded influencers (and the highly connected individuals) who will act as 'real' change agents across all the relevant areas of the organization. This is carried out through an initial ONA. Communications scan combined with a series of iterative meetings/questionnaires where those initially identified as relevant change-positive or open-minded influencers progressively identify others with these characteristics. Computer input and analysis are used during this process, so that individuals who influence/communicate strongly outside their work areas (brokers) can be identified as well as those who influence/communicate with their direct work colleagues. Where computer access is difficult, a manual process can be used, with data keyed in at a later time for analysis. By adopting this iterative process using a very high percentage of change-positive people, you are able to get a very accurate picture, avoiding the high levels of inaccuracy associated with psychometric testing and representative samples – where the views of change blockers and the alienated can severely distort the results.

- Using frameworks to clearly define and agree the 'bounded freedom' boundaries where managers, change professionals, influencers and highly connected individuals may respectively exercise their discretion in driving change forward. These boundaries then form the basis for a series of practical mechanisms that facilitate effective collaborative working between managers, change professionals and real change agents across the organization.

- Using management coaching to build relevant skills and competencies for working effectively in *this* change environment – not just generic skills that do not relate directly to working with other managers, change specialists and real change agents across formal organizational boundaries during a period of ambitious change. Needless to say, practical collaborative behaviours form a major part of this coaching.

INVOLVING MANAGERS AND REAL CHANGE AGENTS ON CHANGE TEAMS

Using selected managers and real change agents in the change programme through involvement and a process called 'reinforcement' (see below) is the middle-layer process of the integrated informal network approach. When using this approach, very few, if any, line managers and real change agents are seconded full time to work on change teams. Work on change teams, steering committees, and so on is very much a part-time activity, leaving the influencers and highly connected individuals with the bulk of their time doing their day-to-day jobs – with lots of colleague contact and opportunities to build wider staff support for relevant change initiatives. Despite being part-time change team members, the managers and influencers chosen for change teams (and strongly supported by senior management) will have a profound impact in four main areas – enhanced change quality and relevance, relevant and timely change communications, successfully pioneering new change implementations and driving agreed culture change.

IMPROVING CHANGE QUALITY AND RELEVANCE

The inclusion of selected managers and real change agents in the change process must be closely integrated with the programme and project management structures – see Figure 4.4. These selected managers and influencers will usually not be skilled in many of the techniques needed for organizational design, process design, systems design, performance management or programme management. They do, however, bring a strong understanding of the current work environment, the strengths and weaknesses of colleagues, and the issues and concerns that are currently talked about in the workplace. In their part-time roles (on change teams, steering committees and so on) they can therefore add a new dimension to the change programme by acting as reality checks on proposed changes, suggesting ways that the proposed new work environment

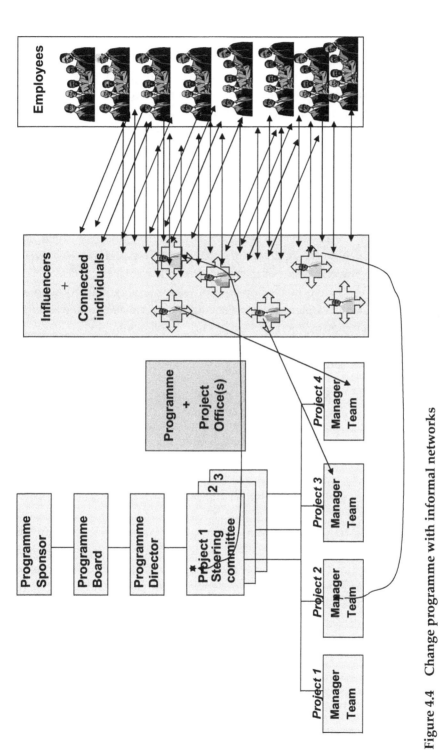

Figure 4.4   Change programme with informal networks

can be improved from a staff and service user perspective, and highlighting potential problem areas.

A very important aspect of this participation is that these managers, influencers and highly connected individuals become more personally committed to the change programme (if they are used as valued members of change teams and not just 'token gestures'). This increased personal commitment in turn increases their impact as change agents, increasing buy-in at both middle management and local staff levels through peer pressure – the people enthusing about the changes are influential and respected by colleagues, they are fully informed on current developments in the change programme and they have strong senior management support. The motivation of the selected individuals is very strong, since their morale is boosted by being chosen for these roles, and their career prospects are likely to be significantly enhanced if they perform well over the change period. The end result of using selected line managers and real change agents in this way is that many potential problems are highlighted at an early stage and dealt with; implementation schedules are adjusted to take account of local 'readiness for change' (ensuring that early implementations are successful, leading to a positive bandwagon effect); changes have practical imperatives built in; and timescales and budgets are much more likely to be met.

RELEVANT AND TIMELY CHANGE COMMUNICATIONS

The overall goals of any change communication campaign are to ensure that people affected by the change programme are aware of the change programme and its aims and buy in to relevant changes in the programme; individuals know how they fit in the new organization; individuals know what is expected from them; individuals are continuously up-to-date and clear about progress being made.

While many traditional communication mechanisms are used during a change process, selected influencers and other highly connected individuals are used throughout the communications campaign to place great emphasis on informal communications and feedback, while still maintaining a high profile and professional approach to formal communications (see Figure 4.5). In effect, the approach focuses on achieving an effective, focused level of 'buy-in' to the change programme through coordination of formal and informal change messages. Levels of buy-in to change by different groups across the organization are monitored informally and at regular intervals (typically monthly) in meetings of the change communications team. This real time communications feedback via influencers and highly connected individuals forms the basis for ongoing monitoring of 'readiness for change', which in turn impacts on change sequencing decisions.

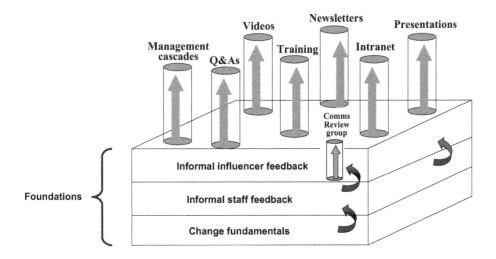

Note: The 'Communications Review Group' is a key channel in bridging informal and formal communications across the organization

Figure 4.5   Change communications: relationships between channels

PIONEERING SUCCESSFUL CHANGES

As a normal part of the change process, real change agents are frequently used to test new training events, new systems and new ways of working. These individuals are trusted to give objective feedback on strengths and weaknesses, and to generate ideas on how things can be improved. There are often situations where new organizational designs, processes, systems and working arrangements need to be piloted before a full roll out of new ways of working can take place. Typically, these pilots are used to test the designs, with relevant improvements being made and used in the full implementation.

Some managers, supervisors and key operational staff have the competencies to pioneer new ways of working, including the ability to overcome teething problems. Wherever possible, these rare individuals should be used to repeatedly establish one new work area after another. Some, but not all of these people will be real change agents. Experience shows, however, that real change agents are an excellent starting point to rapidly identify other staff with these pioneering capabilities.

DRIVING CULTURE CHANGE

Culture change is all about changing the way that people behave in the work environment – not just what they do but the way that they do it. Identical processes and systems can be used by different organizations to deliver very different levels of service to their stakeholders. A stakeholder (say a person from another part of the organization or a member of the public) knows within a few minutes (possibly seconds) whether your organizational culture is essentially pleasant, helpful and efficient or just a hassle to deal with! And this depends primarily on your culture, not just your processes, systems and levels of formal staff training.

It is not possible to impose successful, practical culture change through senior management directives. A broad consensus across managers and staff at all levels is required before people are willing to consistently change their underlying behaviours – for example, being more innovative, more agile, more stakeholder-focused, being easy to work with (rather than difficult), and so on. The first step in building this consensus is to get senior management buy-in to the need for a new culture and the process for making the necessary changes. This will involve delegating considerable responsibility to selected influencers, who will contribute to the creation of the new culture vision and (particularly) its implementation. Although gaining wider management buy-in will be an ongoing process, it starts with one or two workshops during which senior managers (from different locations as necessary) draft a set of practical new behaviours and agree the sharing process required for effective culture change. (Senior managers, moreover, need to be practical exemplars of the desired new behaviour patterns. 'Do as I say, not as I do' is yet another recipe for disaster! A classic example of destructive informal 'permissions' at work – see below.)

At this point, the culture change process is communicated to all staff. Senior managers strongly express their support for the development and implementation of a practical and effective new culture, based on day-to-day behaviours that have the widespread support of both managers and staff at all levels.

During the earlier process of identifying change-positive and open-minded influencers, the key roles of both influencers and managers in culture change is discussed, together with the importance of culture change to the future success of the organization. Getting buy-in from those influencers who volunteer and are chosen to work on culture change is generally very easy. The ongoing process of getting influencer (and staff) buy-in continues with the establishment of a culture change team.

An effective cultural change mechanism is usually based on four main components (as illustrated in Figure 4.6):

1. Group influencers, who are strong local influencers (representative of the different locations) and are by nature change-positive or

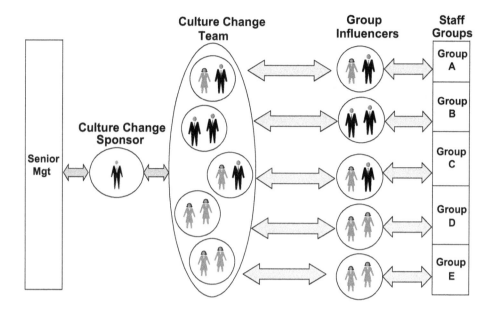

Note: Some of the group influencers are selected for the Culture Change Team

Figure 4.6   Effective cultural change mechanism

open minded, and who have agreed to participate locally in culture change activities.

2.   A culture change team made up of a subset of group influencers, who have agreed to focus their main change activities on culture change.

3.   A culture change sponsor, who is a very senior (often the most senior) manager.

4.   The senior management team.

Driven by the sponsor and an empowered Culture Change Team, this mechanism assesses current behavioural problems; reaches a consensus on desired behaviours; initiates changes in organizational mechanisms to root out destructive behaviours and replace these with positive behaviours; and drives changes in both manager and colleague behaviour through extensive peer pressure.

CARRY OUT EFFECTIVE CULTURE INTERVENTIONS

One of the first activities carried out by the Culture Change Team is to fill in an electronic questionnaire designed to identify and analyze the underlying permissions (the unwritten rules about the ways we behave here) that drive the current culture. This software is based on extensive research into cultural permissions and rapidly focuses attention on potential cultural problems resulting from destructive permissions.

> `Permissions are the unspoken and unwritten messages contained in the design of organisational structures and processes, and the behaviour of individual managers. They signal to people what is, and what is not, acceptable behaviour. "Management communications" are relatively rare events. Permissions, however, hit employees thousands of times every day, literally drowning out the best efforts of managers to communicate a different message.*
>
> *.... permissions are the invisible web of informal communications that sit between the underpinnings and the key dimensions of a high-performing organisation. High-performing organisations do not use "obsessive communications" – they obsessively seek out destructive permissions and convert them to positive permissions, thus solving the communication problem.'*

Source: Denis Bourne, Magus Toolbox.com

As a natural next step in this process, using a software diagnostic tool designed specifically to enable a valid analysis of immediate and root causes, managers and influencers iteratively reach a consensus on desired behaviours that are specific to achieving the new culture. In doing this, they create best practice scenarios and practical examples of both desirable and undesirable behaviours that are currently taking place. Subsequent Culture Change Team workshops (held weekly at first) then refine the potential cultural problems, making them more specific to elements of the current environment, and identifying potential changes to both organization mechanisms and manager/colleague behaviours. This usually results in a specific set of change projects designed to modify and remove some existing organization mechanisms (structures, systems and processes) in order to replace destructive permissions with positive permissions.

CHANGING MANAGER AND COLLEAGUE BEHAVIOURS THROUGH PEER PRESSURE

In several 'waves', location-by-location, influencers and managers (led by the senior management team) then participate in starting the implementation of new behaviours within the day-to-day work environment. Behaviour changes are based on day-to-day 'reinforcements', where positive cultural behaviours are supported and destructive behaviours challenged – usually informally – by influencers and managers as these occur.

Managers and influencers exchange experiences and support each other throughout this process. The numbers of daily reinforcements are measured and, together with experiences, are discussed at the (now monthly) culture team meetings. The most encouraging aspect of these behaviour-changing exercises is that (despite some limited backsliding) positive behaviours become embedded even when the formal reinforcement exercises cease. A key 'permission' – to challenge destructive behaviours and actively support positive behaviours – has been established and is being exercised many times each day in all areas of the organization.

COORDINATING EFFECTIVE CULTURE COMMUNICATIONS

Throughout the culture change project, managers and influencers on the culture change team coordinate both formal and informal communications on the vision, plans and progress made in culture change. Emphasis is continually placed on the importance of very practical new behaviours to the future success of the organization in achieving its key objectives.

All staff are progressively involved in the culture change project through reinforcing behaviours and using relevant new mechanisms on a day-to-day basis. The key message throughout is that culture consolidation through daily behaviour reinforcements is a process that lives on after the formal culture change project ends. Reinforcements may change over time as the culture adapts to changing service needs, but they never stop.

MEASURING CULTURE CHANGES

During the initial senior management workshop(s), the ways in which culture change will be measured are agreed. These measures will fall into two main types:

1. 'Real time' measures (at least monthly) that will guide culture change activities. Typically, these are simple measures – such as 'the percentage of colleagues currently carrying out desired behaviours' on a day-to-day basis – collected at the monthly culture change team meetings, supported by ongoing informal feedback from staff at all levels.

2. Formal measures (at regular intervals, including relevant questionnaires at the start and the end of the culture change project),

based on those agreed by the senior management team, often with a strong emphasis on stakeholder impacts. (An example of how managers and different levels of employees may view current culture is illustrated in Figure 4.7.) As always, the real change agents (selected local influencers and highly connected individuals) will assist with questionnaire design, participant selection and output analysis.

PROBLEM INVESTIGATION AND RESOLUTION

Problem investigation and resolution is the outer layer process of the integrated informal network approach. It focuses on people-related problems that may arise during the implementation of major and continuous organizational change. Questionnaires that attempt to analyze problems or provide insights into how organizations and individuals function have been around for many decades. The big problem with most staff questionnaire exercises in large organizations, however, has been that they usually raise as many issues as they resolve – and seldom drive really effective developmental action. During the research that led to the integrated influencer/ONA approach, one senior HR manager in a large government department made a very serious point when he said:

> 'There is a whole world of well-designed questionnaires and questionnaire-based software out there that has been pretty useless because of accuracy and interpretation problems.
>
> With a typical 70 per cent response rate, we really do not know who the missing 30 per cent are. Are they the bored and disinterested? Or the change-negative people? Or just the really productive people who were too busy doing their tough jobs? Could many of those who fill in the questionnaire be lying?'

The integrated informal network solution to this fundamental problem was to radically improve the reliability and accuracy of change-related questionnaire surveys by focusing on the reliability of those who completed them (even if this means smaller samples of participants) rather than trying to interpret results from an undetermined mix of reliable and unreliable participants in larger samples. The principle used is that (at least for problem investigation and monitoring during major organizational change) a 20 per cent sample from reliable participants, with a 100 per cent response rate, is much better than a 100 per cent sample with a so-so response rate where the participant reliability is unknown. Managers and influencers identified through earlier processes form the core group for most ONA questionnaire exercises. Where a larger sample

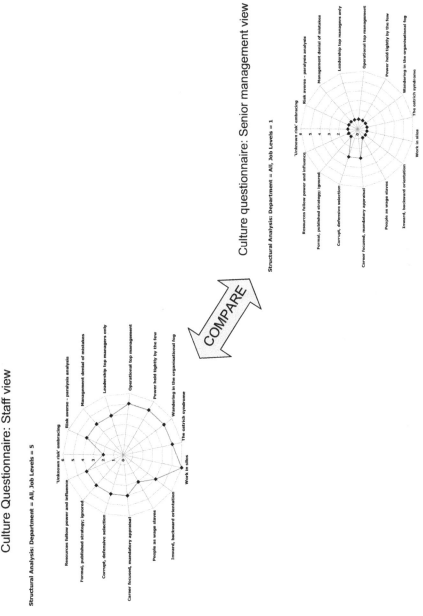

Figure 4.7   Differences between staff and senior management culture analyses

is needed, these two groups are used to identify, convince and guide carefully-selected other colleagues as they complete the relevant questionnaires.

Experience has consistently shown that this focused approach to problem identification and monitoring is highly valuable; particularly since these exercises can often be carried out rapidly where a potential implementation problem has been observed but where the scale of the problem is uncertain. 'Real time' problem identification and rapid resolution are key ONA principles during the implementation stages of major organizational change.

Impact of outsourcing on informal networks

As mentioned in Chapter 1 (The failure of business leadership), managers are typically very poor at implementing business change. Despite professional adherence to change methods and a proliferation of increasingly sophisticated technology and process design tools, the success rates for ambitious business change programmes that impact on how people work day-to-day remains depressingly low. One of the most recent surveys, conducted online by *McKinsey*

A CONFUSING PICTURE OF WHITE-COLLAR OUTSOURCING

If we take the published 'evidence' at face value, white-collar outsourcing is currently:

- *Growing more slowly than in the last few years, but growing at about 5 per cent per annum nevertheless.*

- *Experiencing a surge of activity in some industrial sectors, particularly financial services.*

- *Failing to deliver significant financial benefits in most cases, due to the inherently high costs of the outsourcing model – 10 per cent negotiation/contract costs, plus contract management costs, plus 15 per cent profit margins, plus staff TUPE*

costs, and so on. In many cases, outsource vendors need to increase efficiency by 40 per cent plus before they make any profit.

- *Failing to deliver best practice/ quality/innovation in many cases, as vendors become complacent once contracts are in place.*

- *Failing to deliver flexibility/ capacity/scalability because contracts are binding and (by nature) inflexible.*

- *Failing to focus on non-core business activities, with more than a quarter of all outsourcing contracts transgressing the non-core criteria.*

Inter-personal communication patterns

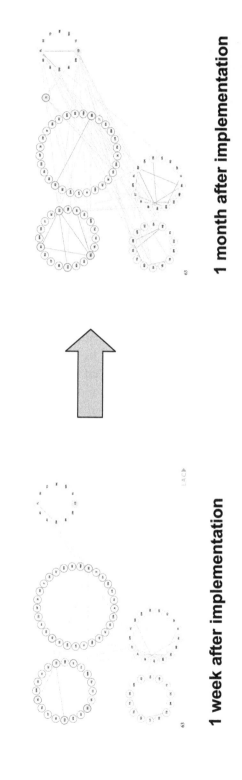

1 week after implementation

1 month after implementation

Figure 4.8   Monitoring change through informal networks

> - *Failing in many cases to provide access to high-calibre skills due to high vendor staff turnover (particularly offshore) and a growing realization by client organizations that the knowledge base they have paid for was fleeting.*
>
> - *Failing to effectively transfer risks to the vendor, since vendors are unable to fully absorb the costs of business losses, often leaving the organization responsible to pay the bill.*
>
> - *Experiencing high levels of 'insourcing' as organizations bring inhouse many of their failing or inflexible outsourcing arrangements.*

Quarterly in 2006, showed that only 38 per cent of global executives reported that the recent business transformations that they knew best had a 'completely' or 'mostly' successful impact on performance.

In contrast, and although their track record is far from perfect, outsource suppliers are much more competent in implementing 'Radical Disruptive' business change that impacts on the way that large numbers of people work on a day-to-day basis. This is primarily because outsource suppliers need to be *much* more efficient and productive than their clients if they are to make a profit on their outsourcing ventures. In essence, they *dare* to be *much* more efficient, and this drives everything that they do. In many cases, however, outsource suppliers are forced to overcome one fundamental hurdle that does not apply if change is implemented without outsourcing – they have to fragment at least some of the relevant informal personal networks! Certainly, with the traditional outsourcing model, the outsourcing supplier's new employees are quite likely to be moved around the organization so that they work for a variety of clients over time. Progressively, this is likely to further disrupt informal networks leading to less flexibility, agility and innovation over time.

So how will current and new outsourcing boundaries be overcome as businesses increasingly seek to harness their informal networks for business benefit? The answer in most cases is with considerable difficulty. Indeed, the constraints on integrating informal networks across outsourcing boundaries will build increasing pressures on businesses to in-source more of their processes and IT resources.

As mentioned in Chapter 1 (The failure of business leadership), much organizational change failure has resulted from the inability to drive change through informal (influencer and highly connected individual) networks:

'Change failure is not usually due to overt 'change blockers' in the organisation, although most change professionals have come across them from time to time. The causes of failure are much more insidious and can be best described as 'death by a thousand cuts' where opposition or indifference is experienced in small ways in many parts of the organization. Bit by bit, the proposed changes get delayed and diluted. Traditional top-down programme and project management almost always fails to address this type of insidious erosion.

The only effective way to address this dispersed, erosive threat is to selectively engage significant numbers of dispersed leaders (influencers and highly connected individuals) and use them to enhance rather than dilute proposed changes, winning hearts and minds of colleagues along the way. This principle applies to all continuous improvement programmes as well as major change initiatives. The trouble is that very few organizations (or consultants!) know how to accurately identify dispersed leaders.'

Because of the fundamental importance of using informal networks to drive successful business change, these increased pressures on outsource suppliers may well shape the future direction of the outsourcing industry. Although the use of informal networks will improve even further the outsourcer's ability to drive business change within their areas of control, pressure from clients (and potential clients) for effective informal networks is likely to limit traditional outsourcing and increase in-sourcing. The end result may well be a fundamental shift in the outsourcing model itself.

Impact of informal networks on outsourcing

The current white collar outsourcing model is one where staff and associated facilities/technologies are transferred to outsource vendors for an agreed price and period of time. Since the late 1990s, Business Process Outsourcing (where entire business processes are outsourced) has become available alongside, and sometimes integrated with, the more mature traditional IT outsourcing model. Often, Business Process Outsourcing is associated with the development of new IT systems (or new IT system platforms) to enhance the ongoing delivery of the relevant process. Although the outsourcing market has grown rapidly over the last decade, aided by increased offshoring to low wage economies such as India, it has not been problem free. Indeed, many of the more optimistic projections for market growth have failed to materialize as a whole range of difficulties have been experienced. In a

VIEWS AND CLUES

The inflexibilities are often negotiated into the (outsourcing) contract by buyers, whose faith in the existence of large cost advantages is akin to a belief in alchemy, according to Scott Scarrott, Compass's head of business development. 'There's no magic,' he says. 'An outsourcer has to be 20 per cent better than the in-house operation just to cover set-up costs and break even. Factor in a margin for risk, overhead and profit and that rises to 40 per cent. That's a handicap that can't be offset by simple "labour arbitrage" even in low-wage countries such as India, where high labour turnover and low productivity compound the disadvantages.'

Source: *Out of house, out of mind – and out of pocket, The Observer*, 13 May 2007.

Skills shortages are a massive problem for the Indian IT industry. *Even though there are approximately 14m graduates in India – almost twice the number on the US labour market, and growing by 2.5m a year – the rapid growth of India's service sector has quickly absorbed much of the available graduate pool.*

The labour situation is so tight that demand for skills will outstrip supply by 2008. Demand has already pushed prices up by 23 per cent a year since 2001, eroding one of India's competitive advantages.

According to a McKinsey study, multinationals think only 10 to 25 per cent of Indian graduates are worth employing. The rest are, employers believe, poorly educated or coming away with irrelevant, non-engineering degrees and poor English.

Source: *Multinationals test small town Indians, The Register*, 1 September 2006

situation where in-house managers are poor at implementing business change and where outsource suppliers are currently experiencing major cost base problems – and facing a future where their model inevitably fractures the efficiency of relevant informal networks – where do business executives and the outsourcing industry go from here?

The most obvious answer is to move towards a very different outsourcing model. A model that solves many of the outsourcing cost problems, while making their change capabilities available to business executives without forfeiting the growing opportunity for integrated informal networks that drive effective business change.

The traditional outsourcing model will be replaced progressively by an in-house 'transform-operate-transfer' model. This form of 'in-house outsourcing service' keeps all the benefits of outsourcing (such as the authority to implement major staff changes, enhance skill sets, change processes and associated systems, and build new business through innovation), while avoiding the heavy costs and risks of complex contracts, staff transfers/TUPE, and contract monitoring/ maintenance. This model is based on the service provider delivering a core team of change design and implementation specialists who will take transitional responsibility for selected areas of the business (typically end-to-end business processes or carefully considered back office functional areas) and will deliver agreed target changes in typically a 12-month or 18-month timescale. The contract will normally be much closer to a simple 'fee plus performance bonus' consultancy contract than to a complex outsourcing tome. But the in-house 'transform-operate-transfer' model does not just advise on change. The supplier is specifically responsible for delivering agreed measurable changes on time and within budget.

Client organizations that make use of the in-house 'transform-operate-transfer' model will also experience significant levels of culture change as many existing management practices based on 'command and control' are replaced by a more collaborative management style. Just as collaborative management is needed to work effectively with influencers and informal personal networks, it is also essential for working well with suppliers delivering 'transform-operate-transfer' services. In delivering these new services, outsource suppliers will need to become experts in using influencers and highly connected individuals, working with ONA scans (as well as with all the formal change approaches) to deliver effective rapid, resilient change. Once the penny drops, they will respond well to this challenge, just as they responded well to the challenge of 'becoming much better at change than their clients' under the old outsourcing model. They will do it because they *have* to if their business is to succeed.

Under the 'transform-operate-transfer' model, technology and project management techniques are likely to be pragmatic, rather than over-ambitious. Large new systems are more likely to be assembled in logical 'pieces', rather than one huge unique central system (as attempted recently by the UK's NHS). These assemblies will be based on suitable technology platforms and the choice of platforms over time will be made pragmatically – avoiding undeveloped elements yet not loitering too long with well-established yet cumbersome software environments; getting the timing right for moving to newly emerging technical platforms – both software and hardware – and using recently developed federated tools to ease the transition. Reuse of industry specific software elements will increase even further in future. Project management methods will increasingly incorporate the techniques for manager/influencer/ highly connected individual collaboration mentioned above and will be very practical, rather than theoretical or purist.

VIEWS AND CLUES

The latest quarterly index from TPI, the outsourcing advisory firm shows that the world-wide outsourcing market declined by almost one-third (31 per cent) when comparing the total value of broader market contracts let in the first quarter of 2007, $17.6 billion (€14 billion) with the first quarter of 2006, $25.4 billion (€20.3 billion). Indeed this year saw the lowest total contract value of outsourcing deals in any first quarter of the past five years.

Duncan Aitchison, Managing Director of TPI, commented, 'Contract awards world-wide have got off to a much slower start this year than traditionally seen in the first quarter, portending a softer outsourcing market for all of 2007, continuing the slowdown of the global outsourcing market which first became apparent in the second half of last year. Whilst, the decline in the total value of deals done is in part due to shorter and therefore lower value contracts, this is not exclusively the case. The US's current reluctance to outsource is also a contributory factor.'

The downturn in overall outsourcing contract activity is exemplified in the decline of Business Process Outsourcing (BPO). 2007 has experienced the smallest number (29) and lowest total value, $2.8 billion (€2.3 billion) of BPO contracts greater than $25 million (€20 million) awarded in the first quarter in almost five years.

Source: Global outsourcing market down by almost a third as US market and BPO slows, FSN Newswire, 30 April 2007

Those businesses continuing to use the traditional 'complete outsourcing' model will focus heavily on 'commodities outsourcing'. Standard product manufacturing will continue to be outsourced internationally, as will a variety of commodity white-collar back office functions (selected finance, some HR, office services and so on) and technology-based services (web-hosting, mass e-mailing, disaster recovery and so on). Despite this, large organizations will increasingly find that they have the economies of scale to keep even commodity services in-house, with medium-sized organizations becoming the main focus for commodity outsourcing vendors. The trend to in-sourcing of IT will also be greatest in larger organizations, particularly as the cumulative impact of using in-house 'transform-operate-transfer' services blows away many of the conservative, bureaucratic cobwebs that tend to grow in larger organizations.

Prediction: As the white-collar outsourcing 'roller coaster' matures, these insights will have a progressively greater effect on the outsourcing realities. Over the next few years (2009 to 2012) there will be many more outsourcing falls than rises as fashion changes and new in-sourcing arrangements becomes as common as – or, beyond 2012, even more common than – new outsourcing deals.

CEOs and senior executives will become much more objective (and much less driven by fashion) in making their sourcing choices. The competence of senior management teams in understanding and working in collaborative ways to implement major change will become a key factor in sourcing decisions. The most effective management teams will be those that can adapt to the challenges of the in-house 'transform-operate-transfer' model. For major business change impacting on large numbers of staff, this approach will yield by far the greatest benefits. Where, however, the senior management team and supporting teams lower down the organization are not equipped or competent to collaborate effectively with contracted specialists in radical, often sensitive, major change programmes, traditional 'complete outsourcing' may be the only viable option. Increasingly, though, pressures will build to replace traditional management teams who are incapable of making the transition to the new, increasingly dominant, in-house 'transform-operate-transfer' model.

Chapter summary

Formal organizations – with all their formal roles and responsibilities, business processes, IT systems and command and control history, can be severely inhibited by conflicting informal personal networks and influencer balances. Similarly, informal 'shadow' organizations – driven as they are by collaboration and personal choice – can be transformed overnight from relatively efficient networks of personal interactions into disconnected demoralized fragments by a few misconceived organizational, process or systems changes.

Both these scenarios are avoidable given what we now know about informal networks. The use of selected influencers and highly connected individuals working alongside selected managers and change professionals can transform the prospects for successful business change of all types. In practice, achieving effective engagement along with effective ego 'smoothing' is often not as difficult as it seems, providing that manager sensitivities are anticipated and reflected during the change process.

Employee engagement is widely touted as a highly effective way to move towards a 'high performance workplace'. However, few if any of the many books and magazine articles on the subject ever address the practical constraints

VIEWS AND CLUES

A government minister ordered his civil servants to draw up a secret list of 'negative' officials suspected of being opposed to legislation.

The instruction was issued by Gerry Sutcliffe, the prisons minister, in an apparent breach of rules that bar ministers from politicising the civil service.

Sutcliffe also wanted a list of officials who could be trusted to act as 'positive champions' for the plans to privatise the probation service and be used to persuade rebellious Labour MPs to change their minds and avert a Commons defeat.

Source: *Revealed: minister orders blacklist of civil servants, The Sunday Times*, 25 March 2007

Organizations that overlook the importance of an appropriate change agent program risk paying a high cost. Consider, for example, an Asian pulp and paper company that created a change agent team to drive its lean-operations program. The group reported directly to top management and was staffed with new hires. However, senior executives failed to recognize and combat the tenacity of the operating group's silo mentality and culture. Plant managers, who held the real organizational power, resisted what they saw as intrusion by a team of young outsiders, leaving management with no choice but to abandon the change program after several months. The change agents could not establish themselves as a credible force in an organization that valued experience and seniority over youth and innovation.

Source: *Building an effective change agent team, The McKinsey Quarterly 2007, Number 4*

– it's just impractical to have all employees engaged on detailed change ideas and activities, all at once. The most effective approach by far is to have a two-tiered approach, where all employees have opportunities to become engaged in idea generation and effective two-way communications, but where selected influencers and highly connected individuals are engaged intermittently at a deeper level.

In practice, a balanced approach is generally the most effective in dealing with potential change blockers. This approach is sometimes called 'the clean sheet' approach. In effect, a key part of change communications is to stress to all affected employees – often informally – that past change-negative behaviour is wiped clean: all employees will be treated fairly and assessed on their behaviours from now on. This does not mean that potential change blockers will be chosen to participate in change activities or as part of change teams. Generally, they will not. However, the 'clean sheet' approach recommends that a limited number of such individuals should be included in change teams, provided always that the balance of numbers/opinions in each team remains strongly change positive.

By using ONA scans, change programmes can create quite efficient informal network configurations operating in favour of change, compared to the largely fragmented and uncoordinated informal environment where potential change blockers are operating. Their influence will 'wither on the vine' in this environment. There really is no need to create 'martyrs' during successful change initiatives.

When relevant senior managers sit down to consider the particular influencers and highly connected individuals to be engaged in business change or product/service innovation, they are themselves being engaged in the change process. This selection process applies a level of management judgement to the raw influencer and informal personal network analyses, builds management support for the process and sets out a framework for empowering the chosen individuals. Specifically, this freedom includes the explicit permission to influencers and highly connected individuals to report bad news to management, as well as good, without fear or favour.

As far as continuous business improvement is concerned, the use of influencers and individuals with extensive informal personal networks will have a profound, positive impact. Even Toyota will become more effective at continuous improvement once they adopt informal networks as an important part of their continuous change toolkit.

Because these informal network techniques focus on the people who should be involved in change and the coordination/enhancement of relevant informal personal networks, they are fully compatible with all established project and programme management methods and with all change design and control methods.

The use of integrated influencer engagement techniques and ONA can be viewed as a series of concentric layers, starting with a core inner layer that determines the people (managers, influencers and highly connected individuals) who will be most effective in driving through the desired changes, on time and within budget. Using selected managers and real change agents in change programmes through involvement and a process called cultural 'reinforcement' is the middle-layer process of the integrated informal network approach. Problem investigation and resolution is the outer-layer process of the integrated informal network approach. It focuses on people-related and other

---

VIEWS AND CLUES

Analyst Gartner predicts the outsourcing market will grow by just 5 per cent per annum over the next few years, a figure far lower than the double-digit highs of a few years ago.

What's more, the analyst says four in every five outsourcing relationships will be renegotiated over the duration of a contract.

Source: *Insourcing vs outsourcing, Computing,* 11 May 2005

Outsourcing is going through 'a mid-life crisis', according to Compass, a management consultancy. When Compass analysed 240 large outsourcing contracts in Europe and the US, it found that fully two-thirds were unravelling before the contract's full term. Far from cutting costs, in many cases outsourcing ended up costing more than keeping the services in-house.

Terminating a contract in mid-term is expensive, but some buyers are finding that the cost of remaining locked in to an inflexible deal is higher still. Sainsbury and JP Morgan are two firms that have scrapped multi-million-pound deals (with Accenture and IBM) over the past couple of years to bring IT operations back in-house; others probably would (and should) do the same, except that they no longer have the necessary expertise to do so.

Source: *Out of house, out of mind – and out of pocket, The Observer,* 13 May 2007

---

problems that may arise during the implementation of major and continuous organizational change.

In many cases, outsource suppliers are forced to overcome one fundamental hurdle that does not apply if change is implemented internally – they have to fragment at least some of the relevant informal personal networks! Because of the fundamental importance of using informal networks to drive successful business change, these increased pressures on outsource suppliers may well shape the future direction of the outsourcing industry.

The traditional outsourcing model will be progressively replaced by an in-house 'transform-operate-transfer' model. This model is based on the service provider delivering a core team of change design and implementation specialists who will take transitional responsibility for selected areas of the business and will deliver agreed target changes in agreed timescales. Just as collaborative management is needed to work effectively with influencers and informal personal networks, it is also essential for working well with suppliers delivering 'transform-operate-transfer' services.

VIEWS AND CLUES

The Japanese economy is recovering from its long slump, but the turnaround may have come at a terrible price: last year a record number of people slogged themselves to death in the workplace.

According to a grim report released yesterday by the Ministry of Health, Welfare and Labour, nearly 150 people lost their lives in fiscal 2006 to karoshi, the postwar phenomenon of death by toil and the phrase most dreaded in the country's ranks of the overworked.

Strokes and heart attacks remain the principal causes of death, although the report noted that overwork-related suicides hit a record 66 cases last year. The near 8 per cent surge in karoshi incidents is a direct blow to Shinzo Abe, the Prime Minister, who came to power last year vowing, among other labour standards reforms, to 'alter the trend of overworking'.

Source: *Downside of Japanese recovery is death by overwork, The Times*, 18 May 2007

In 2002, researchers at California State University discovered that one-in-five employees had engaged in full sexual intercourse with a colleague during working hours.

If further proof is needed that some of us don't always have our minds on the job we are paid to do, another survey found that 15 per cent of American workers spend all day surfing internet sites completely unrelated to work.

Andy Parsley, director of the employee and customer-engagement consultancy Green Lion, says that to pin down what 'employee engagement' means, it pays to think what employee disengagement looks like.

'Last December, a survey by the Chartered Institute of Personnel and Development (CIPD) found that only 35 per cent of people in the UK are actively engaged in their work,' says Parsley.

'But what makes that statistic really depressing is that this is the highest level of engagement ever recorded in the UK.'

Source: *Keeping workers' minds on the job, The Sunday Times*, 25 March 2007

Throwing Out Those Tired Old HR Models

At this point in the book, you might like to consider throwing away all of those old leadership books and all the other worthy tomes that tell you how to design, organize and use people in your business. Perhaps some of the most recent books on engagement and devolved leadership shine some light on reality – rather like walking through your garden at night with a torchlight and noticing your garden shed, pond, rose garden and those weeds that are triumphant despite your intermittent best efforts. Now that the use of informal networks is quite mature, dawn has broken over the HR world. Everything is now in perspective. Established HR practices look very dated and ineffective. It's time to throw out all those tired old HR models, retaining the elements that make sense and building a consistent, invigorating new environment for the people working in your organization.

The 'rules of the game' for employing, engaging, developing, effectively using and promoting people in your business have changed forever. HR professionals working successfully in this new environment will be those who have made a fundamental transition. No longer will they be seen as 'plodders' peddling the latest narrow HR fashion, such as job evaluation, performance-related pay, annual assessments, succession planning, empowerment or engagement. The label of simple administrators of people issues – and difficult situations – will be dead. A pattern has grown up over recent years, in which HR is seen as having one over-riding goal, and that is defensive – the avoidance of industrial tribunals. As one HR executive put it, rather succinctly, 'My job is to keep the CEO out of court!'. HR is at a crossroads – it crucially now needs to work out how it can add serious value to the business. The *real* HR professionals will become the people resource designers, implementation planners and maintenance engineers of *real* 'high performance workplaces'.

Right at the top of their list of objectives will be the key imperative to catalyze and maintain a climate of trust between employees and management.

Without trust it is impossible to build and engage effective informal networks, to create learning organizations or to maximize effective innovation. To carry out this very difficult role, the *real* HR professionals of the future will have to become the influencers who make a profound difference to the way senior managers work with and optimize their people resources. The scale of this task cannot be overestimated. This is not yet another HR fashion initiative. It is a fundamental shift away from command and control to engaging the power of informal networks. The *real* HR professionals who can successfully catalyze this transition (primarily through senior managers and real change agents) will have widespread credibility. Most current HR 'professionals' will fail to make the transition.

VIEWS AND CLUES

In one Hay Group research project on rewards we interviewed several high-level employees at Wall Street brokerage houses who had recently received half-million-dollar bonuses. Several echoed the sentiment of one broker who said, 'Getting the money was great, but it was also a bit of a letdown. What I really wanted to hear was "Thanks. You did a good job." But all my boss did was hand me a check.'

Salary, incentives and benefits are external motivators and rarely give employees meaning. It's not that they're not important to achieving engaged performance. They are. If you don't give people competitive pay, if your company's benefits are sub-par, or if people feel that good performance does not result in higher compensation, they can become disengaged. Perhaps it's best to think of pay and benefits as merely a ticket to the game. If you meet threshold levels for both, you get to play. But you're not going to win the game unless you do a whole lot more...

The more difficult challenge for companies is capturing the hearts and minds of good, reliable employees who are not stars...

Stars tend to be intrinsically motivated to begin with, plus they end up capturing most of the 'prizes' companies offer – the most interesting work, big salary increases, promotions and bonuses. The more difficult challenge for companies is capturing the hearts and minds of good, reliable employees ... who are not stars but who are significantly more productive when engaged.

Research suggests many companies are not succeeding. A huge percentage of ... 'engine room' employees are disengaged. Hay Employee Attitude Surveys show that less than half of them feel they do interesting work. Just one-third feel they can advance, and only about the same percentage feel that better performance will lead to better pay.

Source: *Engage Employees and Boost Performance*, Hay Group, 2001.

As described in the highlights section of this book, for those businesses that successfully make the transition to a sustainable *real* 'high performance workplace', the prize is great:

> *'The use of informal employee networks is maturing. Extensive experience now shows that combined influencer engagement/ONA techniques can be used effectively to manage the people side of change across all types of business change. Successful implementations range from large international mergers and acquisitions, major process and system-driven change programmes, fundamental cultural change and continuous improvement, through to succession planning and employee motivation on a day-to-day basis. The notorious 70 per cent failure rule for business change initiatives is finally dead.'*

As organizations embrace the use of informal networks in their working environments, many of the old, tired HR models from the past will be critically reviewed, changed and often discarded. Once again, it is useful to test these assertions against the strongest, most up-to-date, potentially powerful and fashionable HR concept – employee engagement.

Making employee engagement work

Employee engagement first started to emerge as an interesting concept because of a highly-influential Harvard Business Review paper entitled 'Putting the service-profit chain to work' by James Heskett and colleagues published in 1994. The underlying model described in this paper was in essence very simple: employee satisfaction drives employee retention drives employee productivity drives service value drives customer satisfaction drives customer loyalty drives profitability and growth. Since then the term 'employee engagement' has been widely used but remarkably ill defined. As a rule of thumb, employee engagement can be thought of as the first driver in the above model: So employee engagement drives employee satisfaction drives employee retention drives employee productivity drives service value drives customer satisfaction drives customer loyalty drives profitability and growth. Employee engagement is typically epitomized by high levels of interest in business issues (over and above the 'day job'), high morale, a helpful attitude, willingness to put in discretionary time and effort, flexibility, a willingness to learn and deliver high productivity.

In 2002, The Hay Group carried out a large survey to identify the business value of engaged employees. The results were profound and have been a significant contributory factor to the acceleration of interest in employee engagement in recent years. The Hay survey analyzed the performance difference between 'engaged' employees – those who carried out a range of additional work-related discretionary activities over and above their 'day job' – and 'average' employees. For low-complexity jobs, the performance increase for engaged employees over and above the average was 19 per cent; for moderate-complexity jobs, the performance increase was 32 per cent; for high-complexity jobs the increase was 48 per cent; and for sales jobs the increases ranged from 48 per cent to 120 per cent.

The message was clear in 2002 and has been reinforced by many studies over the last 5 years – engaged employees can transform your business efficiency, service levels and profitability. The only question remaining was how to do it: how to achieve very high levels of consistent, effective employee engagement?

VIEWS AND CLUES

Much of what turns a manager into a leader can be learnt, but not all. 'Good leaders really care and because they really care they expose their true selves and take risks. But you can't teach people to really care and if they don't really care then they are just 9-to-5 jobsworths.' This emotion is at the heart of what differentiates management from leadership, he says. 'Managers coordinate, implement and get things done. Leaders inspire, engage and lift people to higher levels of performance.'

Finally, he (Professor Goffee of the London Business School) advises caution in choosing where you want to lead: 'The irony is that some big organisations say they want more leaders but their structures and cultures often... homogenise people. Leadership is about using our differences and humanity but the organisation effectively kills off leaders and produces suits.' And who'd want to be a suit?

Source: How leaders manage, The Times, 31 May 2007.

Many workers regard annual appraisals as a waste of time, research from Investors in People has suggested.

Its survey of 2900 workers found that 29 per cent of people felt the experience was a waste of time, while 44 per cent believed their appraiser had been dishonest.

Other concerns include managers failing to address issues raised and a lack of continuous feedback during the year.

Investors in People said appraisals were compromised if managers shirked 'difficult issues'.

Source: Staff appraisals 'waste of time', BBC News 24 online, 4 December 2007.

Many organizations and consultancies have tried to achieve the 'holy grail' of effective, high levels of employee engagement in recent years, generally with only partial success. Most of their initiatives used neither selected influencers nor individuals with extensive social networks. Since these initiatives were not using the most effective change mechanisms available, their limited success should come as no surprise. Nevertheless, effective high levels of employee engagement are a key ingredient of a *real* 'high performance workplace'.

Many surveys have been carried out in recent years in attempts to identify the key ingredients for successful employee engagement. For example, a 2005 study of more than 1000 communication and HR practitioners worldwide by Melcrum Publishing found that 36 per cent of the large organizations studied had a dedicated employee engagement programme – with the following top ten drivers of employee engagement being dominated by senior leadership and direct supervisors:

- senior leadership (36 per cent chose as most important);

- direct supervisors (26 per cent chose as most important).

And with less than a 7 per cent rating as 'most important' driver:

- belief in company direction;

- involvement/consultation on company decisions;

- people-centric culture;

- formal internal communications;

- influence over how their job is done;

- understanding of key business issues;

- opportunities for career development

- company values reflect personal values.

ROLE OF SENIOR MANAGERS IN EMPLOYEE ENGAGEMENT

The CEO and senior executives set the agenda for any business. Business strategy and overall business direction are their first priority, in parallel with an effective implementation strategy to ensure that key business objectives are achieved. Too often, senior executives deliver a well-thought-through strategy but with very little idea of how to 'make it happen' in practice. All too often, there is no real commitment and coherent plan to build employee trust in senior managers as an essential high-priority component of the engagement process.

Indeed, trust is such an important issue that it should come first when considering how to achieve consistent effective employee engagement. Building trust is not achieved through a series of planned actions or even a broad commitment to the idea. Neither is it built by management laying off staff as the first action when profitability problems arise. It requires the right mindset and the right management behaviours. Unless the CEO (at least) can commit actively to the following principles, employee engagement will have only a marginal impact in practice:

- Employees are basically bright (irrespective of education level) and the only effective way to treat them is as intelligent adults.

- Always trust employees with the bad news as well as the good. They can cope and inclusion builds confidence. Very few (if any) issues discussed in the boardroom relating to the working

---

VIEWS AND CLUES

The HR community has a habit of identifying an issue, conceptualising it and then developing a variety of different models in an attempt to explain it. The entire process is then wrapped up in HR terminology, largely indecipherable to anyone outside the function. 'Employee engagement' is a current favourite.

In Royal Mail's case it is our front line operational people who know how to do their jobs better than anyone. So it is simple – we ask these people just what it is that prevents them doing a better job. What are the barriers, the blockers?

It is important that we then give these people a boss who knows, understands and supports them, and is also able and empowered to remove these barriers and blockers.

Source: Tony McCarthy, Group Head of People & Organizational Development, *Royal Mail in The Sunday Times*, 25 March 2007

An autocratic or authoritarian manager makes all the decisions, keeping the information and decision making among the senior management. Objectives and tasks are set and the workforce is expected to do exactly as required. The communication involved with this method is mainly downward, from the leader to the subordinate, critics such as Elton Mayo have argued that this method can lead to a decrease in motivation from the employee's point of view. The main advantage of this style is that the direction of the business will remain constant, and the decisions will all be similar, this in turn can project an image of a confident, well managed business. On the other hand, subordinates may become highly dependent upon the leaders and supervision may be needed.

Source: *Wikipedia.org*

environment need to be kept secret from employees. (The informal communications network picks up on key issues very quickly anyway, usually with a few distortions for good measure.) Test yourself: which substantive issues discussed at board level over the last 12 months could not have been shared with all employees within 24 hours? What real value was added by the delay?

- Employees have a key role to play in enhancing and adding depth to the implementation of business strategy. (This does not mean that everyone should be involved with everything but it does mean that everyone should have a chance to express their ideas and suggestions, without fear or favour.) Senior managers (and their consultants) should not try to design every aspect of their proposed business vision in isolation from the workforce. Encourage ideas and involvement in change.

- Be open and honest about the reasons behind the approach that you take to strategy implementation. This is particularly important when describing the use of influencers and informal networks to implement effective change. Managers may worry about working through mechanisms that they cannot fully control, but most employees will welcome them as a breath of fresh air. They recognize reality when it's being used.

- Senior managers make mistakes and change their minds for legitimate reasons. Admit mistakes and say that you have changed your mind. There is often a temptation to post-justify decisions or to put a gloss (spin) on events. Don't be tempted. Always tell the truth to employees – they will forgive errors and poor judgement from time to time, but they will take a very long time indeed to forgive deception. (This is crucial if employees are to be confident in handling the risks associated with innovation. To some degree, *all* innovation is a leap into the unknown.)

- Ideas and suggestions are always judged on their merits and not their sources.

The business leadership should be visible and accessible to employees. Communicating a clear vision of the future is one of the most obvious and important foundations for successful employee engagement. It is the senior management team's responsibility to communicate the high-level business vision to all employees, preferably by CEO presentations in person to all staff. But recognize that this is only the start of a communication and feedback process. Take professional communications advice but veto spin. Avoid marketing gimmicks – did you know that there is almost no example of a change programme that had a flash title like 'into the 21st century', 'time for collaboration' or 'we value our values' actually achieving its business objectives. Both line managers and informal communications mechanisms will build and enhance the strategy over time, with many practical additions (and some subtractions) during the process. Be collaborative as far as possible, take employee suggestions seriously but be comfortable in saying 'no' for the right reasons. Watch out for your ego.

Paradoxically an effective CEO will need to switch between autocratic and collaborative styles at different stages in the process of strategy development through to establishing an effective, engaged workforce to make the strategy real. A typical pattern might be something like:

- An initial level of autocracy when setting out the CEO's broad vision for the future of the business.

- Extensive collaborative work with fellow executives (and others) as the broad vision is altered, refined and extended to clarify the main implications and create a high-level plan of action.

- A second level of autocracy as the CEO makes it very clear that both formal and informal networks will be used in parallel to effectively implement the strategy and to create an environment for future innovation and growth. (Interestingly, this is an example of where an autocratic style is used to drive a required shift towards a collaborative style!)

- More extensive collaboration as the formal and informal networks are evaluated, designed and implemented.

- A bit more autocracy as initial resistance from some (adversely impacted) managers is overcome.

- Ongoing extensive collaboration as the formal and informal network mechanisms gradually move through an initial learning phase and become increasingly effective.

Needless to say, where the CEO (or a large number of senior executives) is not committed and active in driving employee engagement, the results of any engagement initiative will be variable (at best) or just total failures.

ROLE OF MIDDLE MANAGERS IN EMPLOYEE ENGAGEMENT

Although they score very lowly as drivers of employee engagement with the current (usually primitive) approaches, middle managers have a stronger role to play in a work environment that combines influencers and highly-connected individuals with managers at all levels. In future, middle managers will perform a key integration role between senior executives and direct supervisors. Senior executives will set the business agenda, play a major part in building employee trust and establishing the ground rules for implementing the desired new work environment.

Middle managers will interpret and communicate the business strategy in practical terms, influence their subordinate direct supervisors, provide guidance to change professionals, coordinate and act as arbitrators across change initiatives, and ensure that change implementation mechanisms – both major and continuous – integrate and work well over time. If this key role is missing, gaps are likely to occur as change professionals come and go with a variety of projects, a plethora of change initiatives driven by influencers and others may become counterproductive, and cynicism may build up due to a lack of cohesion in business change over time – all this despite high levels of employee engagement and enthusiasm.

In essence, the key role of middle managers will be to optimize the overall integrated – formal and informal – 'business system' that allows employee engagement to work effectively over time, driving the organization nearer and nearer to a *real* 'high performance workplace'. Clearly, the potential impact of some middle managers in carrying out this role will be greater than that of others. Operations managers in charge of large numbers of back office staff, for example, will typically have a greater impact than a middle-level finance manager. Nevertheless, experience shows that even middle-level finance managers can 'punch above their weight' if they become engaged in optimizing the 'business system' rather than just enforcing and administering traditional accounting and budgetary rules.

The time and expensive resources wasted by the budgeting process in most large organizations (mainly outside the finance department) is a huge target for truly engaged finance middle managers to make their mark over the next decade. Another of the big, pervasive issues that operational middle managers will need to address along the road to a *real* 'high performance workplace' will be how performance is measured – the more that performance measures are focused on the 'business system' rather than on individual employee or specific team performance, the quicker business objectives are likely to be achieved.

VIEWS AND CLUES

If service centre (call centre) workers' behaviour is subject to variation, the extent and nature of that variation must be established before any action can be contemplated, otherwise managers will make the situation worse. Managers (and service agents) need to know whether variation in performance is attributable to agents or the system. Current approaches to people management in call centres ignore this important question. The 'sweatshop' sobriquet is a direct result. To hold the worker accountable for performance when in fact it is governed by the system causes stress. Because managers hold them accountable, service-centre workers often believe, as their managers do, that they are wholly responsible for their performance. When they have a bad day they leave work feeling guilty, ashamed and responsible. The organisation has conditioned them to the prevailing philosophy; any agent who questions the philosophy is labelled as difficult or making excuses.

When, as is inevitable, they risk becoming losers, agents 'cheat' – they do anything they need to do to make their numbers. People's ingenuity is engaged in surviving rather than improving performance: a tragic waste of human talent. Agents close a call before the customer is finished, and sometimes before the customer has started; they tell customers to call back, they re-route difficult calls, in short they do all they can to avoid missing work targets or standards. Knowing that they do these things to survive exacerbates their feelings of demoralisation. These are not bad people; they work in a bad system. The human costs of demoralisation are incalculable. The immediate obvious costs are in recruitment and training, since these conditions create high staff turnover. But the real costs are higher – poor service and high costs are associated with customer dissatisfaction and staff dissatisfaction.

Source: John Seddon, *Freedom from Command and Control,* Vanguard Press, 2003, p. 35.

Recent research from the Economic and Social Research Council's 'Future of Work' programme found that more than half of all UK employees – 52 per cent – are now subject to computer surveillance at work. Many of those surveyed reported that stress levels were increased as a result. However, in a decade of working with change-positive and open-minded influencers, our own experience shows that it is not the monitoring itself that leads to discontent. The real problem is the misuse of the performance data by managers.

Typically, this misuse arises because managers focus on individual performance rather than on the performance of the 'business system'. For example, variations in the transactional work carried out in back offices is often underestimated. Managers then pressure individual employees or small teams to 'do better next week' or even 'do better tomorrow' without understanding the impact of variety in the workload. Once managers get used to measuring fluctuations in performance as part of natural workload variations, the problem of misuse of performance data largely disappears. Only by understanding the performance fluctuations inherent in workload variations can individual or team performance begin to be objectively assessed. When this happens, change-positive and open-minded influencers are usually surprisingly supportive. These key influencers are more likely to be frustrated by managers' ineffectiveness in dealing with genuine poor performers than they are to oppose robust actions to remove persistent low performing individuals. Far from being a human utopia in which all human behaviour is accepted, genuine employee engagement has very real boundaries in the tolerance of persistent laggards.

ROLE OF DIRECT SUPERVISORS IN EMPLOYEE ENGAGEMENT

As described earlier, supervisors and other first line managers do the bulk of the face-to-face 'managing' in an organization. It is therefore not surprising that they are secondary only to senior managers as important drivers (or 'brakes') in building employee engagement. Research and practical experience of influencers shows that on average only about 40 per cent of these key local managers are change-positive or open-minded influencers. Although this figure varies considerable between different areas within an organization and between organizations, it begins to explain why success in employee engagement initiatives varies a lot between different organizations.

As the use of informal networks becomes more and more common in modern businesses, the local, first line manager roles will increasingly be filled by change-positive and open-minded influencers. The main exceptions will be new local managers who have potential but who have not been with the organization (or group) long enough to create an effective influence network with colleagues and cross-organizational peers. These exceptions may include individuals with the potential eventually to move into middle or senior management positions, but who are going through a process of gaining practical operational experience. The management styles of these key supervisory influencers are naturally collaborative and this tendency will grow in an environment of extensive influencer engagement. This, in turn, will encourage and accelerate the growth of employee engagement in the organization. Until the mix of first line managers is predominantly made up of change-positive and open-minded influencers, the current mixed pattern of success and failure in employee engagement is likely to continue. However, the trend will be increasingly positive as the practical use of informal networks grows.

VIEWS AND CLUES

Source: *Keeping your best and brightest, CIO Update,* 9 March 2005.

According to the 2004 U.S. Job Recovery and Retention Survey released by CareerJournal.com and Society for Human Resource Management, 75 per cent of all employees are searching for new employment opportunities.

Of those, 35 per cent said they were actively searching, 40 per cent are passively searching, and almost 50 per cent of employed respondents said they will intensify their job seeking efforts as the job market improves.

So, instead of competing for vital talent on the usual competitive salary, nice team-mates, and so on, maybe its time to start thinking about competing on the basis of how the ITO in your company will support your employees optimal business success, while increasing their market value.

Some years back, a comprehensive study of printing companies divided them into successes and failures, using every possible criterion to separate the sheep from the goats. The differences between the two were stark on every issue of strategy and tactics – none more so than on the central matter of ambition.

Asked if they aimed at continuity, profit or growth, 53 per cent of the failures plumped for the first, only 4 per cent for profit, and just 14 per cent for growth. The successes plumped equally for profit and growth, at 46 per cent apiece. Note that the figures of the failures fall far short of 100: 19 per cent of the relative flops had no objectives at all.

Source: *Closing the management gap with strategic objectives,* Robert Heller, *Thinkingmanagers.com,* 8 July 2006.

Interestingly, the shift in first line management skills towards better collaborative and communication skills will have one important, possibly controversial, side effect. As mentioned earlier, over time, more and more first line managers are likely to be women. (The reason for this trend is basic biology. Women's brains are designed more efficiently than men's brains where communication and effective multi-tasking and collaboration are concerned.) Experience also shows that women have disproportionate influence across informal networks when compared to their male colleagues in similar roles.

BELIEF IN COMPANY DIRECTION

Employee belief in company direction is a secondary driver since it depends heavily on the effectiveness and credibility of the senior managers and supervisors doing the strategy communication.

Interestingly, unless the strategy itself lacks credibility (which is rare, since most business strategies – although often incomplete – have at least a reasonably strong logical base) the actual content of the strategy has little effect on whether it is believed and supported by employees. Neither does it matter much whether the strategy contains 'good news' or 'bad news' from an employee perspective. Employee support for business strategy can be equally strong for a recovery strategy as for a growth strategy.

The key deciding factor is a combination of management credibility and how the strategy is to be implemented. A recovery strategy (with all the usual restructuring and downsizing) presented by a failing board with the prospect of ongoing command and control management in future is likely to be greeted with disillusion and cynicism. In contrast, a recovery strategy put forward by a credible new management team and including a fundamental shift from command and control to the use of informal networks, a new breed of influential supervisors and extensive employee engagement has a much greater chance of success.

Nevertheless, the acid test is always what happens in reality – usually in the first 6 to 9 months of any new business strategy. Employee engagement and 'belief' will grow and begin to thrive if managers keep their side of the deal – managers adopt collaborative styles, influencers and those with extensive personal networks are identified and included in change teams, new supervisors move into post, all employees are given opportunities to input their ideas, idea selection based on merit, and so on. If managers, however, fail to establish the right supportive environment or fail in their communications the prospects for belief in the company direction are bleak.

INVOLVEMENT/CONSULTATION ON COMPANY DECISIONS

Traditional consultation through trades unions or staff associations has always suffered from one fundamental drawback – the individuals concerned are rarely strong influencers and where they are, they are often change-negative by instinct. Even today, staff representation often contains elements of these negative undertones, which tend to reinforce managers' command and control instincts to issue directives when consultations get difficult – leading in turn to an increasingly confrontational environment. From time to time, managers may then be tempted to 'sweeten' key individuals in order to minimize conflict, leading in extreme cases to sex and corruption allegations such as those currently embroiling Volkswagen in Germany.

VIEWS AND CLUES

Flexible benefits may be instrumental in attracting, retaining and motivating quality employees, but employers need to measure the effect on these annually and respond to any emerging trends in staff preferences and attitudes if the business benefits are to continue long term.

At the Royal Bank of Scotland (RBS), where the flexible benefits scheme is in its eleventh year, the rewards team has found that employees who elect three or more benefits under the scheme are up to 20 per cent more engaged than other employees. Greig Aitken, head of human capital strategy at RBS, says the company has achieved such results by changing the way it delivers the package. 'We employ around 120 000 members of staff and the take-up rates of flex have been good, but about three years ago we started to think about how we could improve our flex scheme and ensure that it was still meeting the needs of the staff.'

The company undertook detailed employee analysis and recognised that it needed to make changes and offer more benefits under the scheme that were relevant to employees of different ages and those with different lengths of service. 'This helped to engage staff quite individually with the programme, and by 2005, helped to reduce staff turnover levels by 2 per cent, saving the company £60 million,' adds Aitken.

Source: Employee engagement: Refreshing flex schemes creates closer ties with the workforce, Employeebenefits.co.uk, 4 June 2007.

Private sector workers have a greater sense of pride in their workplace and its management. Private sector workers are more likely to believe that their employer knows where it is going and to feel pride in what their organisation delivers to customers and clients than their public sector counterparts.

A survey of almost 1000 UK workers, by Mori's Social Research Institute and the Work Foundation, revealed that 69 per cent of private sector staff felt senior management had a clear vision of where the organisation was going, compared with 61 per cent of public sector workers.

Source: Public declaration of pride in private sector companies, Personneltoday. com, 3 August 2005.

In looking forward to the constructive use of key influencers and informal personal networks, CEOs and senior executives need to consider carefully which business change issues these key individuals should become involved in and which (if any) they should not. While influencer involvement in some key decisions will be constrained by legal and practical constraints (for example, the details of a redundancy exercise or a takeover bid), even these sensitive issues will often benefit from manager/influencer discussions – in advance, well before the specifics need to be evaluated and agreed.

PEOPLE-CENTRIC CULTURE

A people-centric culture is an essential component for a thriving business environment containing high levels of effective employee engagement.

This does not mean, however, that such a culture has to exist now or in the immediate future. A people-centric culture can largely be created in a surprisingly short period of time (typically in 6 to 9 months) by a combination of senior management commitment and the intelligent use of change-positive and open-minded influencers. The use of an effective culture change mechanism (as described in Chapter 4, Balancing formal and informal employee networks) in parallel with key influencer and highly connected individual engagement in continuous improvement and specific business change initiatives, provides a highly effective combination to drive people-centric culture change.

One of the key decisions that will need to be made in building such a people-centric culture is to what degree employee terms and conditions should be tailored to employee needs and aspirations. For example, how should issues such as flexible working, flexible benefits packages, job rotation and personal contracts be dealt with? Should the organization adopt a 'one size fits all' approach or should terms and conditions be tailored to fit the aspirations of different groups, on different sites or located in different countries? There will always be a trade off between aspirations and costs. Both managers and influencers will need to adopt a mature, flexible approach in finding the right balance for your particular organization. This flexible approach will be particularly important where organizations are undergoing periodic upheavals, such as when a business adopts a growth strategy based on multiple acquisitions over a period of (say) 5 or 10 years.

FORMAL INTERNAL COMMUNICATIONS

Although formal internal communications are important in setting out management strategies, objectives, plans and policies, it is the combination of integrated formal and informal communications on a consistent basis that really 'delivers' by increasing employee engagement. As a minimum, informal communications should be facilitated through a monthly communications review group. The objective of this group is to monitor cultural 'permissions', to coordinate formal and informal communications, to monitor employee feedback and to provide guidance into future formal communications.

Communication Review Groups can be set up for each main area of the business or each significant geographic location. These review groups are aimed

> ## VIEWS AND CLUES
>
> *Further in-depth analysis of our NHS case study data revealed that engagement levels can vary, in association with a variety of personal and job characteristics and with experiences at work. Some key findings were:*
>
> - *Engagement levels decline as employees get older – until they reach the oldest group (60 plus), where levels suddenly rise, and show this oldest group to be the most engaged of all.*
>
> - *Minority ethnic respondents have higher engagement levels than their white colleagues.*
>
> - *Managers and professionals tend to have higher engagement levels than their colleagues in supporting roles, although people in the latter group appear to owe greater loyalty to their profession than to the organisation in which they practise their craft.*
>
> - *Engagement levels decline as length of service increases.*
>
> - *Having an accident or an injury at work, or experiencing harassment (particularly if the manager is the source of the harassment) both have a big negative impact on engagement.*
>
> - *Employees who have a personal development plan, and who have received a (good) formal performance appraisal within the past year, have significantly higher engagement levels than those who have not.*
>
> Source: *The drivers of employee engagement*, Institute of Employment Studies Report 408, April 2004.

at rank and file employees, rather than managers. Each review group usually consist of between 15 and 30 individuals, with between 30 per cent and 50 per cent of members being local change-positive or open-minded influencers. Review groups meet monthly to hear management presentations about proposed changes, to discuss communication issues and to feed back information on successes, problems and areas of concern. As a rule of thumb, the number of change-positive influencers should always exceed the number of change-negative influencers to avoid the dangers of the groups being taken over as destructive 'moaning' venues. It is important, nevertheless, that change-positive, undecided and change-negative individuals actively participate in these groups. This 'mixed attendee' policy is often an important element in building credibility for the group, while still ensuring an overall positive outlook.

INFLUENCE OVER HOW THEIR JOB IS DONE

In any effective employee engagement situation, influence over the way that work is done is core to making the engagement effective. Without acceptance of this principle, for example, Toyota would be just another car manufacturer with at best a so-so continuous improvement record.

Employee influence over how the job is done, however, does not mean that all employee suggestions are automatically implemented or that all ideas from change professionals are rejected. The key to success is that ideas are judged on their merits in a constructive, collaborative environment. It is management's responsibility to create such an environment.

Using respected local influencers and highly connected individuals simply makes the creation of a constructive, collaborative work environment much easier.

UNDERSTANDING OF KEY BUSINESS ISSUES

Employees' understanding of key business issues is heavily dependent on the effectiveness of formal and informal strategy and business planning communications. As mentioned above, this starts with a strong executive commitment to building employee trust in senior managers and in the overall business direction. This is an essential high-priority component of the engagement process.

Once again, the use of key local influencers and highly connected individuals in coordinated formal and informal communications and feedback greatly enhances effective communication of key business issues. If management actions, such as the commitment of resources or the use of their own time, is focused on key issues, then the informal messages are strongly reinforced. However, if management actions are concentrated on other issues, mixed signals are sent and employees become confused at best or just cynical and demoralized.

Communication of key business issues to all employees is carried out (intentionally or by chance) through many channels, some formal but many informal. Because employee understanding of key issues is impacted by such a variety of signals, including management actions and attitudes, strategy and business planning communications should always be coordinated effectively. For example, even in situations where senior management actions and behaviours are sending the wrong signals, influencers working on communication review teams should be empowered to feed back their concerns – without fear or favour. Management reactions in these sensitive situations will largely determine the degree of trust that exists between managers, influencers and (therefore) all employees in future.

VIEWS AND CLUES

Employees in China consider non-cash benefits such as 'learning and development opportunities' and 'career advancement opportunities' as the most important factors in determining to join and stay with a company. 'Competitive base pay' is seen as the third attraction driver in China. Employees see 'career advancement opportunities' as the top engagement driver. However, only 41 per cent actually believe their employers are providing such benefits.

At present only 16 per cent of the employees surveyed in China are fully engaged in their work – meaning they are willing to go the extra mile to help their company succeed. 33 per cent are partly to fully disengaged, meaning they invest as little energy as possible in their job, and they are probably actively looking for another job.

In Hong Kong, only 5 per cent of employees are fully engaged, and nearly 60 per cent are partly or completely disengaged.

The gap – dubbed the 'engagement gap' by Towers Perrin – is leading to a high level of mobility and a low level of efficiency among many companies. 68 per cent of employees surveyed in China and 73 per cent in Hong Kong are either actively looking for another job, would consider another offer or have already made plans to leave current job.

Source: *The 2007 Towers Perrin Global Workforce Study.*

The client was a large high street retailer. A major concern was high staff turnover. The company commissioned an assignment to establish the causes, and recommend remedial actions – the cost of recruitment was huge. Two days into the assignment, the two consultants working on the project met to exchange experiences. The next day they called an emergency meeting with the HR Director. It was suggested that an immediate 40 per cent reduction in staff turnover could be obtained, with little investment needed. The Director's initial reaction was amazement and delight at the thought. When asked how, the consultants pointed out that all the company had to do was stop employing permanent staff. When the Director expressed surprise, it was noted that, on average, permanent staff stayed in their jobs for 2.4 months, whereas temps hung in there for an average of 4 months.

Quite apart from the fact that the people in the HR function had not noticed (asleep at the switch again?), an interesting insight was the reason for the difference. The jobs that the employees were being asked to do were dirty, boring and subject to brutal feedback, compounded by extensive security checks to reduce stock 'shrinkage'. In the circumstances of lack of trust, permanent employees found it hard to contemplate staying. Temps knew they were only there for the short haul, and so survived longer.

Source: *Reflections on management lessons not learned,* Denis Bourne, *Magus-Toolbox.com.*

OPPORTUNITIES FOR CAREER DEVELOPMENT

It is a frequent management misconception that opportunities for career development are a common driver for employee engagement, staff motivation and retention. The reality is very different. The importance of career development varies radically between professional and administrative workers, between the old, the middle aged and the young, between males and females, and between different countries around the world. Perhaps not surprisingly, young male professionals and rising executives typically score career development as much more important than older female administrative workers.

However, almost all of the surveys on the importance of career development are based on the results of representative questionnaires – and therefore of variable quality. It is also a common mistake for HR managers to assume that their workforce will value career development (and other HR-related elements) in line with external survey findings. External and internal surveys are certainly useful as guides as to what drives employee engagement, but there is now a better way. A combination of internal questionnaire surveys and key local influencer analysis and insights will provide a much clearer picture of the importance by work area of career development. This approach also adds value across a whole range of other HR issues driving (or not driving) training, motivation, staff rotation, succession planning, retention, and so on.

COMPANY VALUES REFLECT PERSONAL VALUES

Even a brief examination of the employee turnover rates of cold-calling call centres or complaints sections in leading banks shows that people do not generally choose to work for long in inherently stressful environments. Although these are extreme cases because of the frequently confrontational nature of the work, research has shown that where company values do not align well with employee personal values, engagement, morale and retention all suffer.

Although the business models of some organizations inevitably lead to some contentious areas as far as employee values are concerned, each individual's perception of these issues will be largely determined by the values experienced on a day-to-day basis. For example, if (say) a pharmaceutical company has very acceptable work practices, encouraging high levels of employee engagement through extensive use of influencers and informal networks in parallel with good internal communications, accessible, trusted executives and good employment packages, the perceived value alignment is likely to be high. This will apply even for many of the employees who have ethical concerns about

THREE SELECTION PROCESSES THAT DON'T WORK... AND ONE THAT DOES

Selection interviewing: *'Selection interviewing is one of those much-researched subjects, on which the researchers are all agreed – but apparently not too many people are listening to them. The general agreement is that, as a device for predicting performance, the standard selection interview has a just about perfect record – of failure. Yet, in spite of the evidence that continues to pile up, both in the research and through live experiences of practising managers, it remains the most popular method of selecting staff, from entry level through middle managers to top brass.*

This paradox would require explanation if, in fact, there was no effective alternative to the standard selection interview. In those circumstances, there might be a lot of frustrated managers out there, waiting with bated breath for a new technique to emerge, while still struggling with the vagaries of Lady Luck and old methods. The reality is that there are other, more effective methods. Unfortunately, too many people stay wedded to the comfortable routine of reviewing CVs – and asking the standard questions that are so well rehearsed that all too many candidates have their answers lined up just waiting for the opportunity to offer them...'

Competency Analysis: *'What is a competency? What does a competency contain that is additional to and different from three old fashioned words – skills, knowledge and attitudes? If there is no satisfactory answer to this question, it is suggested that the whole subject be dropped, and that attention be given, instead, to concepts that work and demonstrably so.*

Moreover, any methodology that is to be useful to practising line managers has to be subject to measurement and be able to predict performance. Part of a 1965 research project demonstrated that attitudes cannot be measured, and, even if they could, would produce no demonstrable basis for predicting performance.

As a final thought, the attitudes of people at work are partly a vector of their own human characteristics and partly a consequence of the organisational environment in which they think and act. The latter includes the managing style and behaviours of their colleagues, and that opens up an interesting can of worms...'

Psychometric testing: *So, we are left with the overall conclusion that psychometrics do what it says on the tin, providing that we recognise that the reputable purveyors of these packages make only narrow claims for what they assess, and what the results actually mean. Even then, there are the reservations about the reliability of the assessed results. Factor in the bigger question of what we are trying to achieve by using them, at all, and the answer to the question starts to look rather different. If we are using psychometrics for predicting performance, we are going to be disappointed. If we are using them to identify development needs, we are going to be disappointed. If we are using then as a vehicle for developing the performance of our people, we are going to be struggling even more. In other words, for those very utilitarian perspectives, psychometrics do not work. The question is why they should be considered in the first place.*

The Conscious Behavioural Skills model: *The alternative is to use the very well established conscious behavioural skills model (CBS). 'Conscious Behavioural Skills' are those used by knowledgeable*

employees to demonstrably convert their knowledge into effective behaviour, enabling people and the organisation to reach their full potential. It has been around for years; it works; it does not require any mysterious research into the invisible; it supports selection and development applications, directly. The snag is the CBS model is a rather challenging model to apply, for the practitioner. In which case, it is not totally surprising that many employers and their advisers avoid the difficulty and fall back on all the current 'flavours of the month', psychometrics and their like, which at least has a series of very good defence mechanisms in place – ready for the time when things don't quite work out as planned.

Source: Denis Bourne, *Magus-Toolbox.com.*

animal experimentation despite the counter arguments in favour of improved human and animal heath in the longer term.

As mentioned earlier, cultural change in terms of both the practical values and the day-to-day behaviours can be implemented well within a year through the commitment of senior managers and the engagement of influencers and informal networks. Experience shows that most documented organizational values are readily accepted by the workforce, with few if any value changes being made during culture change initiatives. It is at the practical end of cultural change – poor work procedures and the real day-to-day behaviours of managers and employees – where fundamental changes are often needed to drive widespread employee engagement.

A revolution in employee recruitment and succession planning

All the key messages in this book so far call out for fundamental changes in the way that most organizations recruit and promote their people.

Organizations that achieve *real* 'high performance workplaces' will have managers, influencers, highly connected individuals and most other staff capable of high levels of engagement and collaboration. Most but not all managers will also have the ability to make tough decisions and even be autocratic from time to time – so providing rapid decisions and impetus to deal effectively with problems and even the occasional crisis.

A NEW APPROACH TO RECRUITMENT

These two key behaviours – the ability to engage effectively and to collaborate effectively – are almost impossible to identify using two of the most common selection techniques currently used by large and medium-sized organizations – selection interviewing and competency analysis. As stated opposite, while skills and knowledge can readily be assessed in interview and test situations, it is impossible to accurately measure 'attitudes', the third plank of competency analysis.

Fortunately, as well as assessing the skills and knowledge of potential recruits, it is also possible to evaluate their behaviours in what are broadly called 'situational interviews' – based on the conscious behavioural skills model (CBS). This form of interview is based on providing a number of descriptions of relevant, commonly experienced situations, often problems, and asking the candidate how they should be handled. This approach can be used for both internal and external job applicants.

As a first-cut selection tool, the problem situations can be presented via a computer-based web system offsite to weed out the obvious misfits and create a short list for face-to-face assessment. The face-to-face assessment then typically has two components: an individual problem-solving exercise and a group problem-solving discussion. The individual problem-solving exercise is designed to assess suitability to engage beyond the normal job boundaries. The group problem-solving discussion then builds on this assessment, while providing an insight into the candidate's collaborative (or otherwise) behaviours. Supported by the CV, relevant skill/knowledge tests and the views of the assessors, situational interviews provide the most effective means of selecting new employees up to the reference stage, including managers, for your future 'high performance workplace'. Situational interviews are more time consuming and expensive than traditional interview approaches, but they give better results. Your future 'high performance workplace' inevitably starts with your recruitment process, so follow Toyota and get the best employees you can at the recruitment stage – it's very cost effective over time.

A NEW APPROACH TO SUCCESSION PLANNING

Starting at the bottom of the organization, situational interviews can be used to assess current employees who apply for non-management jobs internally. Depending on the job requirements, influencer assessments and informal personal network analyses will also be available to support the selection process. Moving on to succession planning and selection for first line manager roles (including supervisors and team leaders), change–positive or open-minded influencer status becomes one of the key selection criteria. Once again situational interviews are the assessment tool of choice. As a routine element in each internal job change, the relevant individual's informal personal network status will be assessed to identify situations where informal networks may become fragmented by the move, with appropriate remedial action being taken. Better still, contingency planning to build or maintain strong, healthy informal networks should be carried out in advance where key individuals (particularly communication or information 'brokers') have been identified for potential promotions or job rotations.

At middle management levels, current positive influence with those who will become direct reports after the promotion of an internal candidate becomes a key selection criterion. In addition, the focus of the collaboration and the problems in the situational interviews will be on optimizing the 'business system' to create a 'high performance workplace'. Otherwise, the succession planning and selection process is similar to that for first line managers.

At senior management level, strategic level capabilities remain strong selection criteria, alongside a mixed ability to be 'sometimes autocratic but usually collaborative'. Influence assessment should be focused at board and middle management levels.

Moving towards a 'high performance workplace'

Many forward thinkers in today's organizations might well think that if they really want to achieve anything approaching a *real* 'high performance workplace', they would not want to start from where they are now.

A highly-autocratic organization, built up over the years by one or more driven CEOs, is likely to have autocracy imbedded throughout its management hierarchy – after all, these are the behaviours that get rewarded and promoted. Lower level employees in this organization are likely to mainly obey the rules, with all the accompanying stifled innovation, disillusion and eventual lack of

VIEWS AND CLUES

Our research has used well over one hundred thousand questionnaires to track the practices that a company can use to improve its performance—from increasing the leadership's effectiveness and ability in charting a clear course to motivating employees and giving them the ability to innovate. By studying the impact of specific practices on specific organizational outcomes, we show that several popular remedies do not live up to their reputations:

- The carrots and sticks of incentives appear to be the least effective of the four options commonly used to motivate and encourage employees to perform well and stay with a company.

- Applied in isolation, KPIs and similar control mechanisms (such as performance contracts) are among the least satisfactory options for improving accountability.

- Relying on a detailed strategy and plan is far from the most fruitful way to set a company's direction.

- Command-and-control leadership—the still-popular art of telling people what to do and then checking up on them to see that they did it—is among the least effective ways to direct the efforts of an organization's people.

Source: *Managing your organisation by the evidence, The McKinsey Quarterly,* August 2006.

For some years, the HR profession has described itself as being 'at a crossroads', with perennial conferences questioning its future role. The question itself is predicated on disquiet within the HR community of the value of services provided to organisations: do opinion surveys, Investors in People, involvement, competencies, communications, motivational programmes, and so on, actually work?

While these practices may be carried out with good intent, do they really make a difference? Well, yes, but the problem goes a lot deeper. Many if not all of the services provided by HR professionals are based on flawed assumptions or responses to symptoms rather than tackling the disease. It is our underlying organisational theory that is at fault. The pressing requirement is to re-think that theory and in that endeavour the HR professional could and should take a central role.

Our organisations are designed and managed according to the principles and practices of command and control management. Top-down functional hierarchies manage the work, while often being limited to a budget. In a variety of ways, and however we might wrap it up, workers simply 'do as they are told'.

Source: *It's the way we work...not the people, Personneltoday.com,* 16 March 2004.

ambition. Hidden from the gaze of management, there is also likely to be a degree of 'malicious obedience', where employees actively work to make a policy or rule fail, where these do not connect well with their workplace realities. Shifting this type of organization into a modern, innovative informally-engaged business will either require a lot of time and patience, or very significant early changes across the whole management hierarchy. New blood without any informal personal networks on day one will be needed, as well as identifying, engaging and developing your 'most fertile ground' of existing employees. It will not be easy. Nevertheless, you now have the blueprint to develop just such an organization.

At the other extreme, an organization built on a very relaxed attitude to work will have different, but none the less difficult, problems to overcome. Shifting towards a *real* 'high performance workplace' will once again require management changes (and probably fewer employees) to inject a clear strategy and drive at key points in the organization. It will not be easy, but once again you now have the blueprint to develop just such an organization. An overview of how balanced formal and informal networks may be used to create a high performance workplace is shown in Figure 5.1.

Chapter summary

In this chapter, many of the traditional elements of the HR model have been critically evaluated in the light both of the maturing use of informal networks and by considering the evidence of which HR practices work or don't work today. The following HR approaches should either be discarded or fundamentally changed if you are seeking to build a *real* 'high performance workplace':

- all employee recruitment and promotion processes;
- all succession planning processes;
- all performance management processes;
- all leadership training;
- all culture change activities;
- all employee engagement initiatives;
- all internal communication activities;
- most terms and conditions of employment.

And review all the other HR policies while you are at it!

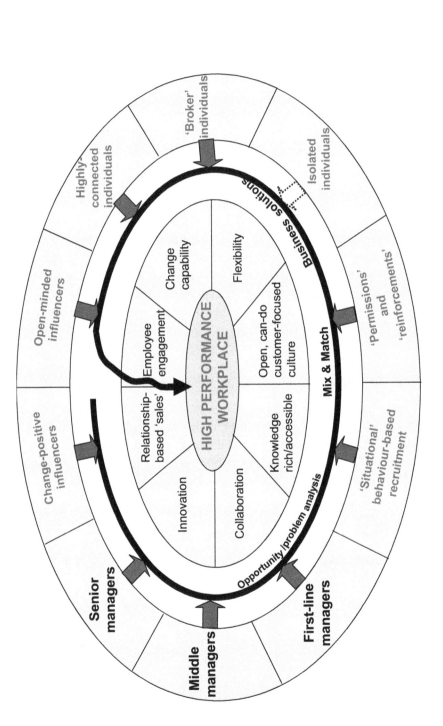

Figure 5.1 Typical informal network options in creating a high performance workplace

VIEWS AND CLUES

Definition: 'The high performance workplace'

'A physical or virtual environment designed to make workers as effective as possible in supporting business goals and providing value. A high performance workplace results from continually balancing investment in people, process, physical environment and technology, to measurably enhance the ability of workers to learn, discover, innovate, team and lead, and to achieve efficiency and financial benefit.'

Source: *The Gartner Group*

Using individual data from the European Survey on working conditions covering all EU member states ... The estimation results unambiguously show that a higher involvement in high performance workplace organisations (HPWOs) is associated with higher job satisfaction ... the results further suggest that this positive effect is dominated by the involvement of workers in flexible work systems, indicating that workers particularly value the opportunities associated with these systems, such as increased autonomy over how they perform their tasks, the opportunity to participate in decision-making, and increased communications with co-workers. Compared to these components of flexible working systems, being involved in team work, and job rotations as well as supporting human resource practices appears to contribute relatively little to the increased job satisfaction from being involved in HPWOs.

Source: *High performance workplace practices and job satisfaction: Evidence from Europe,* Thomas K Bauer, IZA.org, August 2004

Like a jigsaw puzzle without an overall picture, managing people in business has been difficult. The early pieces – built on command and control – were little more than guesses and instinct without any picture to act as a guide. Gradually, command and control has been modified over decades to include delegation, career development, performance management, KPIs, programme and project management, social network analysis, employee engagement and primitive attempts to build the 'high performance workplace'.

But still the results are very patchy. Most organizations struggle to beat the 70 per cent failure rule for profound, people-disruptive business change. Surveys show that most employees are still disengaged from their work. Innovation is sluggish and agility elusive. Harnessing the hidden potential of your workforce has been a slow, often painful process.

But, suddenly and despite the hype, the 'high performance workplace' picture is coming together. The last five radical pieces are ready to be put in place:

1.   Executive leadership – develop strategic direction, with a little autocracy and a lot of collaboration for implementation.

2.   Middle managers – coordinators and enablers for the 'high performance workplace', guiding and integrating a plethora of ideas and initiatives, mainly from below, all within the context of an agreed business strategy.

3.   First line management – the *real* people managers in the 'high performance workplace' – most will be key influencers, so some 60 per cent need to be replaced – often with more women than men.

4.   HR Managers – a key role, to inform and guide senior managers in optimizing the people resource through formal and informal mechanisms – but most won't make the transition.

5.   Local influencers and those with extensive personal networks get much bigger roles across all forms of business change – as these key individuals become the *real* change agents.

For all businesses that aspire to achieve a 'high performance workplace' in which efficiency, innovation, high employee engagement and high morale all combine to form a 'hot spot' of achievement, enjoyment and satisfaction – it's time to throw out those tired old HR models.

VIEWS AND CLUES

More than 1000 public organisations in England (including schools, hospitals, health care trusts, prisons, fire brigades, social services departments and whole local authorities) were officially labelled as failures between 2001 and 2004. 'The extent of failure varies markedly across local areas, some of which have no failing organisations whereas others have more than twenty,' says researcher Professor George Boyne of Cardiff Business School. 'But, in view of these figures, public service turnaround is clearly an issue of pressing practical as well as theoretical importance. We need to understand why public organisations fail and why some are more successful than others at achieving a turnaround in their performance.'

Source: *How to turn public sector organisations around, Economic & Social Research Council, The Edge, Issue 19, 2005*

...The alternative is to get consultants to provide advice on the very product they are about to *sell, which may be a little tricky. Or you might just see what what everyone else is doing or reading or talking about – and do it. Of course, you might take a more radical step and ask the workforce what they think ought to be done – but what do people who produce the things you sell know about anything? No, far better to see what the rest are doing and do it. Unless, of course, they are wearing flared trousers.*

Source: *Chapter on 'Managing (Management) Fashions', Fuzzy Management,* Keith Grint, Oxford University Press, 1997

Knowledge creation:

... knowledge transfer largely dominated early knowledge management initiatives, however, the creation of new knowledge has increasingly been recognised in terms of its ability to provide firms with competitive advantage. Western management has historically focused on 'explicit' knowledge, or hard data and facts, whereas the focus of their Japanese counterparts has been on exploiting tacit knowledge. It is this focus on tacit knowledge, and the resultant superior expertise at 'organisational knowledge creation' that has led to the general success

of Japanese organisations (Nonaka and Takeuchi 1995).

It is suggested that the interaction between explicit and tacit knowledge, which forms a knowledge spiral, is where (new) knowledge is created. Explicit knowledge is shared through a combination process and becomes tacit through internalisation; and tacit knowledge is shared through a socialisation process and becomes explicit through externalisation.

Under the circumstances, knowledge integration is believed to offer the more effective solution to creating sustainable competitive advantage through a knowledge management application. Unlike knowledge transfer, it does not rely on people needing to know everything each other know. The value in knowledge integration is in the meshing of the different knowledge held by individuals. Moreover, through the process of knowledge integration, mutual learning takes place, which means that the total learning achieved is often greater than the sum of the individual parts.

Source: Judith Pierce, *'Knowledge management' – its potential to contribute to sustainable competitive advantage,* MBA Dissertation, 2002.

Managing Your Business Using Informal Employee Networks

Over the decades, there have been many management ideas and theories that have been propounded by a whole variety of inspirational speakers at conferences around the world. Once the initial buzz died down, most of these ideas came to be seen for what they were – mostly marginal improvements on best practices or just an interesting idea that time, and the realities of the business world, forgot. Many were actually very old ideas, dressed up in a shiny new suit of clothes to make them appear attractive – and make their proponents lots of money.

The fundamental idea behind this book is that business can best be managed by a balanced implementation of formal and informal networks. The formal networks are represented by organization charts, business processes, systems and formal procedures. The informal networks are made up of an array of networks: influence networks, communication networks, knowledge networks, varying subnetworks of acceptable and unacceptable behaviours, and many more. All previous business designs have been based on management control through formal networks alone. For the first time, CEOs and senior managers can design and build their organizations by trying to optimize both the formal and informal elements – by getting the balance right.

If, therefore, the concept of managing your business through a balance of formal and informal networks is to succeed – with all the profound changes that this fundamental shift implies – it must be worth it. It must be *much* better than current practice and last the test of time. In other words, if balanced formal and informal networks are to have a lasting and major impact on businesses, the approach must successfully address and resolve most (if not all) of the really difficult problems experienced in businesses today.

To illustrate the power and scope of the balanced networks approach, the first part of this chapter is focused on a wide cross-section of business problems that might confront a new CEO taking over a failing business.

Although the examples used are from the private sector, almost all of the techniques and approaches used can be applied just as well to business problems in the public sector. Further into the chapter, six business transformation examples and a further eight examples of business problems from both the public and private sectors – many with 'invisible' underlying causes – are resolved by using insights from carefully selected influencer and ONA scans.

Using balanced networks to address problems in a failing organization

Consider an extreme case – a new CEO, recently appointed to sort out a failing organization with multiple problems. On day one the CEO has no informal network of contacts, does not know the management team well and certainly does not know who drives all those informal influence networks across the organization. The CEO gets lots of input and advice from direct reports but has little other than instinct to assess the value of this type of contribution. It is, after all, quite likely that many of the senior managers were involved in creating some of the problems in the first place.

If the multiple problems in the organization are reasonably typical, these might include low productivity, poor innovation, a sloppy, error-prone and cynical culture, some effective and some poor managers, poor knowledge and expertise management, and very mixed performances across sales/customer servicing areas. Overall, the organization's track record in making effective changes will leave a lot to be desired.

CREATING THE NEW CEO'S PERSONAL NETWORK

Addressing all these issues will take considerable skill, careful timing and judgement. The CEO will probably call upon consultants, selected managers and others to put together a vision of the future business and a high-level plan for the transformation. The chances of making these proposed changes real are vastly enhanced if informal network techniques combining influencer engagement and ONA are employed. The most immediate benefit is to identify an effective personal network of key people that the new CEO can engage with to drive change. In addition, relevant ONA scans will provide the CEO with a informal network 'toolkit' that can selectively be used later to aid the solution to specific business problems (as described below).

CHANGING THE MANAGEMENT TEAM

Top of the list will be those few individuals in the current management team who are identified as competent, change-positive or open-minded influencers, followed by change-positive influencers at lower levels in the organization. Early, informal discussions with these key influencers will rapidly enable the CEO to identify areas of serious concern and key managers who may need to be replaced. Although some of the existing managers will be capable of playing a part in rebuilding the business, experience shows that significant changes to the management team (at all levels) at an early stage are strongly associated with successful turnarounds.

In choosing new members of the management team at different organizational levels, the CEO should consider promoting change-positive influencers with the right skills and knowledge, as well as selecting new managers from outside the organization. In a failing organization, it is important that changes at first line management level (where most people management takes place) are carried out quite rapidly following the creation of new senior and middle management teams. In all cases, relevant situational interviews, based on face-to-face and team collaborative behaviours, are the assessment tool of choice. Key selection criteria for new members of the management team at different levels should include:

- Senior management – able to develop the strategic direction, with a little autocracy and a lot of collaboration for sponsoring implementation through the organization's *real*, mainly local, change agents.

- Middle managers – able to act as collaborative coordinators and enablers for the 'high performance workplace', guiding and integrating a plethora of ideas and initiatives, mainly from below. (Ideally, all internal candidates should be highly influential with those who would become the new manager's direct reports.)

- First line management – the *real* people managers in the 'high performance workplace' – as many as possible will be change-positive or open-minded influencers, recruited internally, but some will need to be recruited externally – typically, with more women than men being chosen on merit.

As a routine element in each internal job change, the relevant individual's informal personal network status should be assessed to identify situations where informal networks may become fragmented by the move, with appropriate remedial action being taken (see overleaf).

Once the new management team at all levels is in place, each of the business problem areas can be addressed. A wide range of problems is examined below to illustrate how balanced formal and informal network techniques can be used to drive real business benefits in difficult circumstances.

LOW PRODUCTIVITY (AND A POOR WORK CULTURE)

Low productivity is always a symptom of more fundamental, underlying problems, such as poor, disjointed processes, unsuitable (inadequate or over-complex) IT systems or a 'lazy' work culture. Informal network techniques can be used to boost the business impact of traditional process and IT redesign initiatives – which are often very logical but disappointing when implemented – in three main ways:

- By using relevant change-positive and open-minded influencers to refine high-level visions, designs and plans, so that these become more realistic and effective. These key individuals not only understand the realities of the current work environment, but are the most likely group of employees to be innovative and open to new ideas. In addition, they are capable of winning the hearts and minds of colleagues, so smoothing and speeding up the implementation of new processes, systems and work practices.

- By being very selective in deciding on the employees who will be offered redundancy during any (compulsory or voluntary) downsizing exercise. The key to a successful downsizing is to be left with the 'right' people to successfully operate in the new smaller, streamlined work environment. Informal network techniques can be used to identify employees who should be retained in two ways. The most obvious are the change-positive and open-minded influencers. In addition, however, all employees with strong desirable ONA characteristics should be included, providing that they are not identified as 'value-subtracting' or habitually change-negative. For example, those with strong informal communication networks (particularly broker types), key players in innovation or knowledge networks, or those who form a significant role in sales networks (possibly through their extensive contacts with current or potential customers).

- By using selected local managers, working with change-positive and open-minded influencers, to agree new work behaviours and then change the day-to-day culture through a series of 'reinforcement' exercises over a period of months. (As mentioned earlier, reinforcement changes behaviour on a day-to-day basis when these key individuals consistently congratulate and publicize 'good' colleague behaviours when the desired behaviours are carried out. Equally, but less often, they politely but firmly chastise 'bad' behaviours on a one-to-one informal basis.) It won't deliver 100 per cent cultural utopia but it will eliminate almost all of the really poor behaviours very quickly. Effective culture exercises of this type can give a new impetus – a second surge if you get the timing right – to ongoing business transforming initiatives.

POOR INNOVATION

Research and development projects fail more often than they succeed. Out of every ten R&D projects, five are flops, three are abandoned and only two ultimately become commercially viable.

Most organizations with a poor track record of innovation assume that practical new ideas come from a few geniuses or from specialist teams who work in isolation for long periods before submitting their best ideas for review. Even when cross-silo teams are put in place, these are often merely a reflection of internal silo structures – with project leaders chosen because of their seniority or perceived technical ability. These individuals, moreover, may not be the best judges of new ideas, and their specialist expertise may in fact blind them to innovations in other areas. Many will have relatively poor informal networks of relevant (internal and external) personal contacts.

In contrast, the reality is that most innovations are created through networks – groups of people with complementary skills (sometimes at diverse locations) working together. The best innovation comes through problem solving; the best problem solving comes through cross-functional working. Innovation, with its high risk of failure, occurs at the boundary between stability and chaos. Informal networks operate at that boundary, and hence are a good environment for innovation. ONA can be used routinely to provide key insights into those individuals who should best be engaged in different types of innovation – balancing the needs for including key skills within manageable numbers of people, with a range of personal contacts covering all relevant skill and knowledge areas. Frequently, lower level individuals with broad experience within and outside the organization prove to be more effective in innovation teams than their more senior, technically focused superiors who are less well travelled. In large organizations, the ONA databases can be used rather like an estate agent – to bring together the best match of skills and personal contacts to meet the requirements for a specific innovation project. As a rule of thumb, strong personal networks should cover both technical specialists and key managers in the organization who are instrumental in bringing innovations to market.

Once the best mix of individuals is identified for a particular innovation project (or group of related projects), a certain amount of ingenuity is also required to create an optimum mix of formal and informal channels through which these people can stimulate engagement across multiple personal networks – workshops, intranet interest groups, shared database access, social events, mentor arrangement, and so on. Getting the right people engaged in innovation is of course just part of the end-to-end, idea-to-market process. Effective innovative organizations still need to have effective processes in place to rapidly select, test, refine and bring new ideas to market.

It is easy to underestimate the potential impact of this fundamental shift in perspective – from 'specialist groups' to 'complementary skills plus personal networks'. The bottom line, however, is that a very different group of people become involved in innovation, with very different ways of working, and generally with very different, much improved business benefits.

POOR KNOWLEDGE AND EXPERTISE MANAGEMENT

Not all innovation across organizations is large, strategic or organized through project teams. A lot of specific, piecemeal innovation happens as a result of changes in the business or work environment, as part of continuous improvement programmes, or through local initiatives. Many larger organizations have in recent years invested significant sums of money in the development of knowledge management systems and associated training. Some of this knowledge sharing is, from time to time, invaluable in many types of business innovation. A lot of it is redundant.

Now that mature ONA is available, the historic model for knowledge management is changing. The traditional model was typically based on software facilities that enabled the acquisition, organization, storage and dissemination of knowledge content. Generally this was done using standard taxonomies (classification and data relationship schemes) within customized software tools and repositories. The additional (and sometimes alternative) elements in the new model of knowledge management can be summarized as:

> 'Connecting to the right people just-in-time, accessing their knowledge
> and advice on a particular business issue or problem, synthesizing that
> knowledge and applying it to good effect'.

Sometimes this may be formalized through special interest or ad hoc groups, but often it is carried out by one or two individuals working to sort out a problem that looks like it could grow into something bigger.

Once again, the bottom line is that very different people become involved, with very different ways of working, and generally with very different, improved business benefits.

VERY MIXED PERFORMANCES ACROSS SALES/CUSTOMER SERVICING AREAS

Rather like the myth of the genius researchers driving innovation, the myth of the 'super-salesperson' persists in many businesses today. Dig a bit below the surface, however, and a familiar pattern begins to emerge. The reality once again is that most high-performance sales teams operate through networks – groups of people within customer organizations, within the sales team itself and within the parent organization.

Diverse, good quality client connections across several members of a sales team drive better, more focused customer service and enhanced cross-selling opportunities. The most consistently effective sales teams have a broad spread of well-connected salespeople, in contrast to less consistent teams where success is often heavily dependent on a few individuals with extensive personal networks. The most significant benefit of personal networks within the parent organization is to access key information and advice to assist with specific sales opportunities.

Given these insights, the challenge is to recruit only suitable salespeople who are good at collaborating in teams; extending the depth and breadth of existing networks within and across customers and sales team members; extending networks within selected areas of the parent organization; setting up suitable mechanisms to encourage and reward all relevant personal networks; and progressively building the best practices across all sales teams.

The bottom line is that the new CEO will end up with a very different set of sales people, working and rewarded in different ways, delivering increased sales of current products and services, but with both procedures and a collaborative culture that can identify a better range of relevant products and services for the future.

ASSESSING THE NEW MANAGEMENT TEAM

In any new management team – even a team that is selected by the best available techniques – there will be a few 'weak links'. These will be individuals who fail to thrive in the high-pressure atmosphere of a business turnaround – people who feel swamped by the challenges, rather than invigorated. At about 6 months into operating the new management set up, the CEO will be very aware of both high performance managers and those who may need to be replaced. Influencer engagement techniques and ONA can once again provide two key insights into the effectiveness of the new management team.

The first insight is to identify those senior and middle managers (at the 6-month milestone) who are not now viewed as either change-positive or open-minded influencers and who have been identified through recent ONA scans as 'isolated', 'energy draining' or 'value-subtracting' in getting work done or solving problems during the transition. Generally there will not be many of these failing managers but nevertheless it is important to take the necessary action at a reasonably early stage to maintain the credibility and momentum of the key change initiatives. (Care must be taken in assessing individuals in this way because many senior managers can be very effective at a strategic level, or as heads of small specialist areas, without showing up as strong communicators or influencers.) Nevertheless, poor managers in key positions become very visible through these analyses – a perception that can be readily confirmed (or qualified) by informal off-the-record discussion with relevant local change-positive influencers.

The second insight is to identify those first line managers who are change-positive/open minded and influential with their peers and subordinates. As mentioned above, most supervisors/team leaders should fall into these categories at the 6-month milestone. In particular, however, some of the external recruits at supervisor or team leader levels may be failing to make an impact and will need to be replaced sooner rather than later.

Also at the 6-month point, informal feedback from influencers and comparative ONA scans (snapshots of relevant informal networks before and after important changes) will give a sound assessment of how well transitions are taking place and any areas for concern and remedial action. 'Real time' measures of employee support for particular change initiatives on (at least) a monthly basis – obtained from selected influencers on the communications review team(s) – will provide important inputs into change scheduling decisions, as well as highlighting issues and work areas that need to be addressed.

RATIONALIZING BUSINESS LOCATIONS

In many business turnaround situations, downsizing and product or service rationalizations present opportunities to restructure business locations. Relevant

ONA scans showing 'as is' against 'should be' networks for communications, knowledge sharing, interest groups, and so on will often provide essential insights into where connected groups of employees should be located. Rather than indulging in simplistic 'organization chart plus management views'-based decisions, these informal networks open up opportunities for increased interaction between groups where this is really needed – and where there will be significant, indirect business benefits.

Changing the physical location of relevant employees will increase opportunities for important informal contact. In some cases this might tip the balance on site locations in favour of fewer somewhat larger sites. (For example, as mentioned in Chapter 3, Chrysler brought all their people involved in new car development back into one location.) In others, it might simply mean relocating relevant staff from different groups onto the same open-plan floor or redesigning communal areas and communal services. When planning for increased, relevant informal contact, easy access to social areas and facilities can be an important stimulus to an effective informal network design.

Examples of major business change using informal networks

Traditional programme and project management methods have been very weak at managing the people side of change. Where 'user representatives' have been involved in change teams or on steering committees, the people chosen have typically been nominated by local managers, rather than being selected because of their influence or their extensive informal personal networks. Most of the time, therefore, the potentially most useful individuals have been left on the sidelines. In six notable major change programmes, however, – five in the UK and one worldwide – traditional programme and project management methods were combined with the use of selected influencers and ONA scans to very good effect.

MAJOR BUSINESS CHANGE 1: A FUNDAMENTAL IT SYSTEMS UPGRADE AT A MAJOR BUILDING SOCIETY

The change programme was for a major IT infrastructure and associated new application systems implementation exercise for a major building society. During this assignment, the informal networks consultants prepared a management of change strategy and established a practical management of change framework for implementing more than £130 million of new IT facilities that would enable new ways of doing business – through e-commerce and call centres, as well as through traditional branches. This involved working with the outsource supplier responsible for overall programme management by balancing formal and informal networks during all aspects of the change process including change sequencing, communications, training and gaining the commitment of key influencers throughout the organization.

This implementation was so successful – on time and within budget, with widespread staff support – that the building society agreed to the publication of a case study of the assignment by the Wentworth/Gartner Group to illustrate 'best practice in managing a major IT change project'.

MAJOR BUSINESS CHANGE 2: A MAJOR BUSINESS TRANSFORMATION FOR A LARGE GOVERNMENT AGENCY

The single biggest Private Finance Initiative (PFI) contract issued by the UK Government at the time involved a practical partnership between a large government agency involved in finance (investment assets £60 billion) and a leading business process outsource supplier. Under this contract, the outsource supplier runs all the administrative systems and processes for the Agency, as well as taking over responsibility for some 4000 staff. The objective of this PFI was nothing less than to create a highly effective, automated and modern organization that can fully meet the current and future needs of the Agency, while at the same time utilizing surplus staff and a comprehensive IT/IS infrastructure to service new business clients. The technology involved includes e-commerce, call centres and intelligent document scanning and recognition.

The informal networks consultant was in charge of the people side of this massive change initiative, reporting into the change programme director. Part of this responsibility was to guide the extensive work on new organization design, including all aspects of organizational structures, career progression, performance assessment and rewards. The work done represented the leading edge of change management at the time, placing a strong emphasis on influencer identification and involvement, as well as selected ONA scans – and played a major part in the smooth transition of Civil Servants into a highly-competitive commercial business environment. Productivity improvements of more than 100 per cent were achieved while more than 99 per cent of key performance indicators were met during the crucial transition period.

The UK National Audit Office used this implementation as an example of success in PFI implementation.

MAJOR BUSINESS CHANGE 3: A MAJOR BUSINESS TRANSFORMATION FOR A LARGE CITY COUNCIL

A large city council in the north of England and a major Business Process Outsource supplier entered into a joint venture BPO agreement whereby a new organization would run many of the administrative operations of the city council. These included revenues and benefits, IT and human resources.

Influencers at all levels across the organization were identified at an early stage and used to drive all aspects of change communications – both formal and informal – during the critical transition period. The new organization's call centre has subsequently won awards for outstanding performance and the highly automated HR operation has been the subject of many visits by professionals across both the public and private sectors. 'Customer' satisfaction ratings increased significantly. (This major transformation was used as an example of successful technology-driven change in the influential Gershon Report, commissioned by the UK Government.)

MAJOR BUSINESS CHANGE 4: A MAJOR BACK OFFICE TRANSFORMATION FOR A LEADING INSURANCE ORGANIZATION

An innovative Business Process Outsource supplier entered into a business process outsourcing agreement to run the entire back office operations for a major insurance organization.

An associated major change programme led to productivity improvements of more than 25 per cent in operational areas over a period of less than 6 months. The use of influencers and highly connected individuals in the new operations management/supervisory team and for informal/formal communications led to staff support levels for change bouncing back to a higher level than they were 6 months previously. It also led to profits jumping from zero to £10 million+ in the first financial year of the new operation. Many new outsourcing contracts have been won to run different aspects of insurance transaction processing for external organizations, including a significant international insurance contract. Key performance indicators were consistently met during the transition period.

MAJOR BUSINESS CHANGE 5: A CULTURE CHANGE INITIATIVE FOR THE IT DEPARTMENT OF A MAJOR INSURER

The IT Department at a large insurance company embarked on a radical change initiative to transform a relatively traditional IT department into an internal 'commercial IT service' that really treated the business as its customer. This change required organizational, process and internal charging changes that were implemented efficiently over a period of 6 months.

However, it rapidly became evident that a radical change was needed to the culture of the IT group – relationships with customers, the way that new processes were implemented in practice and (above all) the way that IT staff behaved in their day-to-day work. The informal networks consultant led a 9-month programme of practical culture change, using 'waves' of managers and influencers to identify and then progressively 'live' and measure the new desired behaviours. The end result was a profound and measurable change in 'the way that we do things here': Feedback from influencers in the culture change team reported staff 'living' the new behaviours on a day-to-day basis progressively rising from 18 per cent to 55 per cent. Once it became clear that day-to-day behaviours were *very* important, a range of other quarterly staff surveys (over the next two years) vividly illustrated the knock-on effect of real culture change:

MAJOR BUSINESS CHANGE 6: CHANGE TO A GLOBAL STRUCTURE FOR THE IT DEPARTMENT OF AN INTERNATIONAL PROFESSIONAL SERVICES COMPANY

A multinational professional services company created a unified global organization for its IT function, replacing three regional IT groups. Annual ONA scans were used to assess collaboration levels across the world before the reorganization and for two years after the reorganization. The results of the scans highlighted both management and collaboration problem areas, which were then addressed to improve worldwide cohesion, year on year.

The original three-region organization suffered from multiple duplicated functions, dispersed IT leadership reporting to regional executives, limited collaboration on process and technology, and varying levels of service and costs for technical solutions.

In year two, ONA scans showed that connectivity had improved considerably, particularly between expertise groups, but that more collaboration was still needed and the changes in organization and leadership had a limited impact on day-to-day work practices and cultures.

By year three, the ONA scans showed that considerable improvements had been made. Information sharing within all expertise groups and hierarchies had risen by a third. Silos within each region were beginning to disappear, with much better horizontal information flows. Information 'brokers' (communicating strongly across the old regional areas) who were mainly at director level in year one, are now outnumbered by 'brokers' at first line manager levels. Only one of the three original regions continued to have serious fragmented personal network problems. The flow of positive energy increased notably across the great majority of peer groups.

Solving eight different organizational problems using ONA scans

Once an organization begins to use ONA scans to solve practical problems, the scope is surprisingly large. For the first time, managers and influencers can systematically address serious problems with 'invisible' underlying causes. The following eight real life problems were resolved by the use of balanced formal and informal networks:

PROBLEM 1: REMOVING OBSTACLES TO CHANGE

Problem: A highly-bureaucratic corporation was introducing a high and increasing level of innovative technology. Levels of organizational inertia were high and new competition, from smaller more agile companies, was threatening the survival of the business.

Result: ONA scans highlighted the dominant role of two departments, not concerned with technology acquisition, along with a disconnect between these and the rest of the organization. After much debate, involving people from many parts of the organization, four major streams of work were identified, and resourced by 'small armies' of volunteers (who had previously been suppressed by the bureaucracy). Many human and procedural blockages to the adoption of new technology were uncovered and removed or minimized. The competitive position of the business improved. Previously suppressed innovations were released.

PROBLEM 2: IMPROVING TEAM WORKING ACROSS FUNCTIONAL BOUNDARIES

Problem: The general manager of an NHS Trust was concerned that a perceived lack of team working across functional boundaries was a potential source of a reduction in standards of patient care. He was also concerned that there was a lack of focus in the management team on identifying and fixing organizational problems, of which the 'team working' issue was but one example.

Result: ONA scans showed that there was a major lack of communication between ward and community-based nurses about patients' care needs, caused by a small group of consultants regarding information as a source of power. The two groups of nurses fixed the problem themselves, acting informally. The clinical director (who was responsible for the consultants) expressed surprise when the management team pointed out the evidence that he was not acting as a senior manager. (He was persuaded that his desire to be a clinical researcher did not justify his director's salary.) He agreed to change the focus of his attention, including sorting out the power issues involving the consultants. The two groups of nurses, supported by other staff, then rejected the executive's strategy for change, on the basis that it was not radical enough. A reworked, extended and more ambitious strategy got their unanimous support.

PROBLEM 3: REPLACING A FAILED FORECASTING PROCESS

Problem: Over a period of time, the company's performance in managing its forecasting, ordering, manufacturing and distribution network had deteriorated to the point where sales, costs and customer service were all suffering. The major concern was that, having a product with a limited shelf life, getting levels of stock in distribution that were higher than needed by the market resulted in stock write-offs. If levels were too low, then customers could not get the stock they ordered, and needed to satisfy their own customer demands through other sources.

Result: ONA scans and subsequent workshops showed that small variations in the accuracy of sales forecasts had resulted in a degree of 'second guessing' by marketing. Where the second guess proved to be no better, over time, production planning started second guessing the marketing forecast. When the production output did not meet distribution's need to meet customer orders, a complaint went through to sales about their forecasts. Discovering the drift in the numbers contained in their forecast, sales started 'adjusting' their forecasts to compensate for what they thought was simple drift. This generated a whole new round of second guessing, which ended up having a life of its own. Making very explicit what was actually happening drove management action to simplify the whole forecasting/ordering system to eliminate the possibility of second guessing. Stock losses and back-listed orders both reverted to normal levels.

PROBLEM 4: IMPROVING SAFETY IN AN ENERGY COMPANY

Problem: The company was a major player in the energy industry. Their health and safety (HSE) function had come to be regarded as one of the leaders in its field. The head of HSE had, however, become concerned that compliance with rules had become the major driver of behaviour in the operational units, rather than seeking a safer working environment. The role of HSE was seen as a 'police officer', and not one of adding value. Therefore a new initiative was implemented to shift the HSE focus from compliance to value-added to the business. Two years later, an ONA scan was designed to establish the degree to which the initiative was successful, and to identify what was needed to complete the shift to a value-added focus.

Result: The ONA-aided review identified areas of great success, and a priority listing of areas where further attention was needed. More importantly, the work to complete the process was jointly agreed and set up between HSE and operational people during the ONA workshops – a cross-functional programme, as distinct from HSE acting alone. An important and unexpected side effect that also developed through the workshops was a challenge to long-held assumptions about what produced safety in the industry. A new focus on engineering design resulted in a sharp drop in the number of reportable incidents over the next 5 years.

PROBLEM 5: STANDARDIZING PRODUCTS IN A 'HIGH SERVICE LEVEL' INSURANCE COMPANY

Problem: The company provided financial, insurance-based products to two main markets. The first was major manufacturers of high-ticket-price products. These were sold to end users by the manufacturers under their own brand names. The second was through over 22 000 small dealers direct to end users. These were sold under the financial services company's own brand name. New EU regulations meant that the major manufacturer market was going to be opened up to much competition. It was in this market that the insurance company had become the market leader, largely based on extreme levels of customer service, providing highly customized products. The company was weak in the 'small dealers' market, which was where the future growth potential existed. The MD doubted the ability of the organization to handle the degree of change implied in the needed change of focus.

Result: Carefully designed ONA scans highlighted the dominance of certain non-sales and non-marketing functions. Similarly, scans showed that the extreme level of customer service survived only because of the superhuman efforts and achievements of one individual in operations. This was evidently not sustainable under the new conditions expected within 2 years. As a direct result of these insights, sales and marketing developed a new, menu-based system for customizing quotes and new packages. This took about 90 per cent of the effort out of that stage of developing new business. Also the MD changed his own pattern of intervening with key accounts – this provided much-needed time and space for account managers to negotiate more standardized deals.

PROBLEM 6: THE ROLE OF HQ FUNCTIONAL DEPARTMENTS IN OPERATIONAL DIVISIONS

Problem: The organization was a county police force, with a recently appointed assistant chief constable. One of his major concerns was an apparent confusion within the management teams of operational divisions about the role and contribution of HQ functional departments. Seeing an opportunity both to clear up the confusion and rationalize the HQ structures, (with a possibility of cost saving), he commissioned selected ONA scans.

Result: The workshops that routinely accompany ONA projects revealed all the sources of confusion between operational units and HQ, as well as clarifying the exact nature of the problems themselves. A number of revised supplier/customer relationships were worked out during the sessions, based on two-way processes where each member of pairs of parties were both supplier and customer. A side effect, that was not expected, was that a complete layer of management was removed from the organizational structure, as the only identifiable role for that group was that of 'internal banker'. As was noted, 'The job could be done by a relatively junior employee from the Finance department.' The resulting cost savings were substantial.

PROBLEM 7: REVIVING A NEW PRODUCT DEVELOPMENT PROCESS

Problem: The organization was in the business of designing and building engineering products that were sold to other manufacturing industries. Over a period of time, the company had gained considerable competitive advantage through its ability to get innovative new products to the market, on time and in budget. This left its competitors in the position of always playing catch up. The problem was that in the 2 years before the ONA project was carried out, new products had started to arrive in the market both late and over budget. The competitive advantage was rapidly eroding, and the drop in performance had resisted all conventional attempts to fix it, including a couple of goes at re-engineering the new product development process.

Result: All the information generated demonstrated that the new product development process was generally in good shape, with marketing driving it, as hoped. There were, however, high levels of frustration and wasted energy devoted to trying to implement 'house rules', known as 'compliance with protocols', that had arisen through the company's efforts to meet the requirements of a variety of new employee Health and Safety and product liability legislation. The difficulty stemmed from the fact that the protocols had been written by a small, dedicated department in the company head office, whose members had little appreciation of the realities of R&D, product testing and manufacturing. What evolved through the ONA workshops became known as the 'zero references metric'. All departmental heads in the engineering functions in the organization had the same target – 'no references under any of a list of regulations'. Hence safety became a line responsibility, and the head office department was disbanded. Rapidly, the new product development programme got itself back on target.

PROBLEM 8: RATIONALIZING POLICE RESOURCES

Problem: Another county police force was facing a demand for an increased presence on the streets to combat higher levels of burglary and robbery, especially by youths, at the same time as the requirements of new legislation coming from the Home Office demanded an increase in resources in support functions. Needless to say, at the same time, there was downward pressure on budgets. The new chief constable, who had used ONA scans in another force to help develop a new IT strategy, applied a balanced formal and informal network approach to the problem.

Result: The ONA application demonstrated high levels of duplication between functions, gaps between functions and resources applied to processes for which there was no identifiable customer – internal or external. The ONA workshops revealed that this condition was generating a significant degree of frustration among those officers who felt, quite correctly as it turned out, that they were engaged in roles that had no real purpose. The net result was approximately 220 police officers returned to operational policing, with a consequent improvement in crime management. Hence the winners were the community, the organization and the officers who returned to what they had joined the force for in the first instance – to make a difference.

CEO support for a balanced formal and informal network approach

In many ways, it is easier for a new CEO to turn round a failing business using informal employee networks than it is for an incumbent CEO or senior manager. New CEO's have no illusions about their personal networks on day one and are therefore more likely to welcome these new techniques – even if they are outside their normal comfort zone.

In all of the situations described above there was senior management support for the use of balanced formal and informal networks to solve difficult, sometimes intractable, organizational problems. Senior management mindsets, however, are the single greatest obstacle to using informal networks. Often this is simply because they do not have any experience of the techniques and their effectiveness. After all, 'Why should I change the way that I have managed up to now? My career has been very successful without all these new intangible ideas.'

An existing CEO has a lot of historical baggage to deal with. Many have managed to convince themselves that they know who the key people are across the organization. After all, is this capability not one of their ingrained management skills? Command and control type executives are pretty certain that their instincts on employees are correct. Even those senior managers with an open, easy-going, collaborative management style often believe that they know most of the main organizational 'players'. But they are all wrong. This can come as a shock. Senior managers typically recognize only about 10 to 15 per cent of the real local leaders. Even first line managers/supervisors/team leaders struggle to recognize one in three of the critically important change-positive or open-minded influencers. The accuracy level is even lower when managers are asked to identify those with relevant, cross-silo or inter-organizational personal networks.

Quite apart from these issues, another question is always lurking in the background. Who are the potential leaders, who would rise to the surface if the organizational culture was different? These are the people whose natural drives are suppressed, and who seek an outlet outside the organization. They are the, often informal, leaders in clubs, associations and other social groups.

Chapter summary

Slowly the use of informal employee networks is maturing. Extensive experience now shows that combined influencer engagement/ONA techniques can be used to effectively manage the people side of change across all types of business change. Successful implementations range from business turnarounds, large international mergers and acquisitions, major process and system-driven change programmes, fundamental cultural change and continuous improvement, through to organizational problem solving, succession planning and employee motivation on a day-to-day basis. The notorious 70 per cent failure rule for business change initiatives is finally dead – at least for those who embrace informal networks.

Balanced formal and informal networks are particularly good at addressing a wide range of organizational problems with 'invisible' underlying causes. Where change-positive and open-minded influencers are engaged to drive, guide, interpret and build support, the results are particularly effective.

Senior management mindsets are the single greatest obstacle to using informal networks. Often this is simply because they do not have any experience of the techniques and their effectiveness. Sometimes, it is just fear of the unknown. Where CEOs have the courage to embrace informal networks, they will have one underlying source of comfort – more and more, they will not be alone.

VIEWS AND CLUES

Chemistry is the magic mixture of emotions, intuition, and attraction that sparks bonds between us in business, life and love. In the awesome laboratory of life, chemistry is that intangible energy that makes friendships sparkle, marriages sizzle, professional partnerships prosper, and teams triumph.

Chemistry is the most powerful component in relationships because it provides the initial spark when we click. Either you have it or you don't: chemistry cannot be fabricated. And the only way to measure it is with a very unscientific hunch: you know it when you feel it.

Source: *Click – 10 Truths for Building Extraordinary Relationships*, George C Fraser, McGraw-Hill, 2008

Appendix 1: Using Informal Networks – Questions and Answers

Over the last decade, during which the use of influencer engagement and organizational network analysis (ONA) has matured, many questions have been asked by involved managers and employees at all levels. In this section, the most frequently asked questions have been answered – without fear or favour, and certainly without consideration of political correctness. When answering such questions in tense business change situations, you will need to be more empathic to both the situation and the individuals asking the questions. The words used will almost certainly change as a result, but the underlying logic should still be useful.

Questions on 'gaining commitment'

Question: What do you do if the chief executive supports influencer engagement and organizational network analysis (ONA) in principle, but places constraints on what you can do?

   Answer: You can live with some constraints but not others. For example, CEO preferences on which (additional) managers or influencers attend workshops, requests for secrecy/confidentiality of the network details and insistence on some favourite elements being included in the business strategy can usually be accommodated – unless there is a strong balance of executives and/or influencers against specific change proposals. Fundamental constraints, however, such as not identifying influencers or using them in the change process or as guides for ONA exercises are not acceptable. Remember that the real issue is always the success of the business. Be very accommodating on incidental issues, but politely resolute on the 'non-negotiables'.

Question: How do you respond to criticism from some quite senior managers that they have not scored well on the influencer analysis, even though they profess to be fully in support of the business strategy and change plans?

Answer: If you have done the influencer analysis professionally, you will have a high degree of confidence in the resulting influencer list. There is a whole range of messages that can be used to explain why senior and middle managers do not score highly – the main ones being that new managers will not have had time to build up their influence networks and that employees are mainly influenced by people they work with on a day-to-day basis. Just be careful to ensure that all senior managers and key influencers are very clear about the strength and accuracy of the approach. Ensure that the balances of influencers to others involved in the change activities remains healthy.

Question: How do you know that the business vision is at the right level for effective change management?

Answer: This is essentially a matter of personal judgement. Sometimes you will need to move ahead into the change initiative without a vision at the level of detail that you would like. Often, these deficiencies are not critical to the overall outcome – indeed some flexibility is often useful. Nevertheless, where the vision is so vague, or where there are very serious disagreements about major chunks of the vision, you may have to call a halt and recommend a fundamental rethink. Bear in mind that the influencers can be used to drive through change even when a majority of the executives and senior management are opposed. The implications of a radical change approach might be that there needs to be some very early 'bloodletting' at very senior levels – a course of action that should only be contemplated where there is a very committed chief executive and a balance of top-level political power for this radical step change. When thinking about vision, note that a certain degree of vagueness is not only tolerable, but also useful. Long-range strategic plans have little value: a 'roughly west' sense of direction allows adaptive responses to a changing environment to be developed. This is emergent strategy.

Question: Why are influencers a better change management technique than other techniques, such as simple interpersonal communication mapping or Force Field Analysis?

Answer: Essentially because influencer-based techniques are much more focused on the real 'levers' of informal power, particularly during periods of radical people-disruptive change.

When comparing influencers to interpersonal communication mapping, the signal and noise analogy is a good one. The simple communications mapping approach measures all interpersonal communication, including 'noise' from the gasbags who have little real influence. Influence analysis techniques measure the real 'signals', particularly in identifying who is influential and who is pro- or anti-change. However, carefully considered communications mapping (for example, where the questions focus on the frequency and importance of agreed communications) can be very useful both in selecting the best possible change agents in 'cold spot' areas (where there are no influencers) and in providing important ONA scans for diagnostic purposes.

In contrast, Force Field Analysis identifies the 'driving' and 'restraining' forces within the organization that need to be addressed during a change programme. It is, therefore, highly compatible with the influencer engagement approach once influencers have been identified. Generally, it is a poor alternative method for identifying influencers.

Question: If rumours spread that there is a black list of change-negative individuals, what should you do?

Answer: Never create a black list. While it is inevitable that change-positive influencers and others will mention some of the high-profile change-negative people, this information should always be treated informally. It is useful to be prepared for possible opposition and disruption but all individuals should be treated fairly.

Question: When working with the real change agents (selected influencers and highly connected individuals), your access to rumours about the behaviours of various colleagues, managers and executives will increase substantially. How should these be treated?

Answer: You probably won't be able to avoid gathering such information if you have succeeded in building close informal relationships with your real change agents. Mostly, this will be minor salacious gossip and can readily be ignored. Occasionally, however, you will be in a position of having incomplete information of serious concern. On these occasions, it may be worth discussing the issues 'off the record' with the CEO or HR Director so that they are pre-warned of possible difficulties ahead.

Also, as part of the cultural change work that you may be involved with, behavioural reinforcement will directly confront unacceptable behaviours at all levels in the organization. These issues should then be addressed, fairly and impartially, irrespective of the seniority of the person concerned. This is all part of building a climate of trust.

Question: How do you avoid a situation where change specialists and the real change agents disagree on the key aspects of change? What steps should you take if this happens?

Answer: This is a real risk, particularly since the background and experience of these two groups are likely to be very different. The most effective way to avoid disagreements is to establish the roles of the design specialists and the change agents very clearly at the beginning of the process. What are their different but complementary contributions to the success of the project? What should they be, and where is that different from what we have now?

Design specialists are there because of their specific design skills (in organization, process, systems and job design). They typically have dared to think the unthinkable and have succeeded in having (many of) their ideas adopted in other businesses. They must be given this freedom in the current change programme and their ideas must be respected, even when these are more radical than the change agents may have expected.

Real change agents are there because of their business knowledge and because they are the people who will play a major role in making the subsequent implementations a success. They will be undergoing an educational and learning process during the change design stage, and patience will be needed by all concerned. Their considered views, however, must not be overridden or ignored – they are the acid test for what is and what is not achievable in the real 'high performance workplace'.

If disagreement persists despite a clear understanding of their respective roles, you must facilitate a pragmatic compromise. Where you suspect that individual change agent views may not be representative of broader change agent opinion, bring in additional change agents to break deadlocks.

Inevitably, however, the end result of, for example, the organizational design exercise will be a result derived from compromises between conflicting pressures, while ensuring that the main business benefits remain intact. These pressures can be driven by a variety of different factors that can be illustrated as in Figure A1.1 – this type of figure, by the way, can also be used to resolve conflicts.

Question: In the modern electronic age when e-mail speeds up the informal flow of information across an organization, is there not a danger of the informal network having an even greater impact (sometimes destructively) than expected? Are we playing with fire?

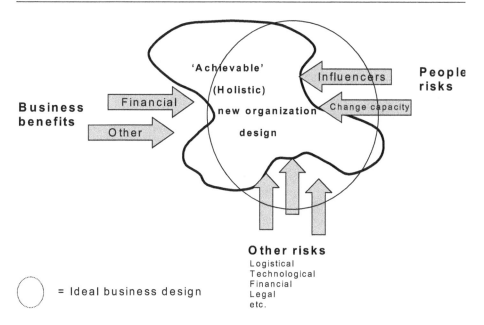

Figure A1.1 Pressures determining an achievable new organizational design

Answer: Yes, we certainly are playing with fire! The informal business communications network is powerful during uneventful times, making and breaking reputations very routinely. During periods of people-disruptive radical change, however, the impact is even greater. Hugely disruptive and expensive change programmes can be thrown off course.

In these circumstances, the choices are to leave well alone (as most traditional change management approaches do) or to intervene and try to achieve key change objectives (as described earlier). Evidence so far strongly indicates that skilful intervention can achieve a lot and that non-intervention is a much riskier proposition as 'death by a thousand cuts' takes hold and change blockers are free to operate unchallenged across rumour mills. Just don't expect the ride always to be a smooth one. As one change practitioner said in an inspired piece of expectation management for an assembled senior management team:

> 'It will be a difficult journey and I will often return to you with arrows in my back from the change blockers and the fearful. Have patience as I ask you again and again to take them out. As you do so, just be thankful that the change blockers have to fire their arrows in the full light of day and not from the shadows. We may lose the occasional battle, we may all emerge with some scars, but we must win the war.'

The bottom line in all of this is that informal networks exist. They form and change spontaneously, and are not management inspired; they are also beyond management control. So, either you find out more about them and why they exist – and enable them to work more effectively, or you stay in ignorance of them – and ignore them. The former route gives you a fighting chance of them being on your side; that latter has very little. Ignorance is not always bliss!

Question: How do you work with internal communications staff to whom much of this approach will be unfamiliar?

Answer: Educating key internal communications staff in the need for coordinated formal and informal messages during the change programme is an early priority. Gaining their commitment is even more important. Early ONA scans will give a good indication of how easy or difficult this task will be – beyond this, it's up to your judgement to resolve any difficulties. Avoid conflict but make sure that the coordination takes place. In extreme cases, limit the internal communications team to purely the formal messages and handle the informal ones yourself in parallel. Work with them to check that formal communications are not contradicted by symbolic messages. Take feedback from employees on this topic. Check the unspoken messages in the design of formal structures and processes, and in the behaviour of senior managers. If, for example, they all emphasize the critical importance of the bottom right-hand corner in the accounts, formal communications about the need for enhanced customer focus will cause more resentment than support for the change.

Questions on 'influencers and highly connected individuals'

Question: Will we necessarily find influencers and/or highly connected individuals in all areas of the business?

Answer: No. In some areas, particularly the smaller ones, there are sometimes just none of these key individuals. Even in quite large business areas, there may be very few. These are important insights that feed into the readiness for change analysis, change sequencing, change monitoring by area and 'hot spot' interventions.

Question: How many people typically need to be interviewed in a work area before the new names mentioned dry up and we can have confidence on accuracy levels?

Answer: Often the plateau effect of fewer and fewer new names being mentioned is discernable at about the 10 per cent level of the relevant population. Typically though, confidence in accuracy levels is obtained at about the 20 per cent level.

Question: What should you do if the influencer identification process delivers either many fewer or many more influencers than expected?

Answer: If numbers are surprisingly low, first ensure that you have carried out sufficient interviews to achieve the plateau effect with confidence. If in doubt, extend the interview process to increase the number of influencers identified. (Take care to ensure that autonomous subgroups are clearly identified. For example, in some large technical areas, relatively small teams work in very autonomous ways, with little influence being exerted across teams. In these situations, a much higher number of interviews are needed before a clear picture of work areas and associated influencers is achieved.)

If the numbers of influencers identified are still surprisingly low, ensure that you are carrying out the interviews in a constructive atmosphere – if in doubt bring in another influencer engagement practitioner of a different sex/ age/background/accent to overcome any obvious cultural problems. Identify any 'personality' problems early to avoid building antagonism, particularly amongst natural change supporters. Don't feel too personally bruised in these situations – no individual or consultant is universally loved by all work groups – but if the problem persists, use someone else to carry out the exercise – influencer engagement is sensitive work and not suited to everyone.

Where influencer numbers seem surprisingly high, there are two possible explanations. Either, there are genuinely a lot of influencers in the particular work areas examined – if so celebrate, and use them appropriately during all (major and continuous) change initiatives. Or you have been too vague/ generous in communicating the definition of change-positive or open-minded influencers. In either case, revisit previous interviewees (preferably on a one-to-one basis) and get them to prioritize the identified influencers using a (say) 1 to 10 weight scoring approach. This will enable you to identify the real key influencers from amongst the other less influential individuals.

Question: What should you do if an identified change-positive influencer is later identified as change-negative (by other positive influencers) during work in a change team?

Answer: If individuals are being deliberately disruptive, then remove them from the change team. But take care. Remember that change-positive influencers were chosen because they were change positive *by nature*. This does not mean that they will always agree with every aspect of a particular change initiative. Indeed, it is one of the strengths of the approach that local influencers will bring very practical insights to the work, leading to improvements in the design of changes, as well as driving the implementation. If individuals are just expressing views that are different from the rest of the team, without being disruptive, then keep them on the change team. Wherever possible try to avoid alienating such individuals – remember that they are still influential and you really do not want to create a powerful enemy of change.

Question: How should an identified change-negative influencer who is obviously trying hard to change and adapt to the evolving new world be treated?

Answer: Change-negative influencers (and highly connected individuals who are change negative) are not necessarily excluded from change team positions, although they should meet the necessary, impartial skills/knowledge assessment like everyone else. In reality, very few individuals have the ability to change their views sufficiently to become real assets in the new world business environment. The few that do have an exceptionally strong drive to succeed. Remember that change-negative individuals can only be included in change teams where the balance of influence on the change team itself is strongly change-positive.

Question: Can you always get all the essential information needed to assess 'readiness for change' in a particular area?

Answer: No, and within reason it does not matter. Just be aware of what you don't know (particularly in small, cold spot areas) and expand your knowledge as your own real change agent network improves. Major delays in gathering readiness for change information may be a symptom of more fundamental weaknesses in your personal approach and these will need rapid correction.

Question: What should the ratio of real change agents to other staff/change specialists be on a typical project team?

Answer: Generally, follow the guidelines of the change management method in use on the particular change programme. Programme and project managers usually have quite strong opinions on these numbers/ratios and you should leave well alone unless you believe that a project manager is 'way off beam'.

However, and it's a very big however, you must always ensure that there is a change-positive balance in each and every change project team. Those with the necessary skills but undecided on the merits of the change programme are acceptable, as is the occasional change-negative individual to placate political pressures. But these individuals must always be outnumbered by the change positive.

Question: Can you give some more examples of how formal and informal messages can be different, yet compatible?

Answer: Yes, and there are lots of examples to choose from. One example of informal messages supporting and adding to a formal message might be:

The formal message is that staff will be freed up for work on new business opportunities through the use of new systems and processes. This leads to staff doubts that the new business opportunities will in fact materialize, reduced by an informal message that the whole cost model of the business assumes that it will materialize and that very senior managers jobs depend on this – so it will happen come hell or high water.

One example of an informal message that spells out sensitive angles on a formal announcement might be:

The formal message is that there are a new set of organizational values and associated behaviours that will gradually be adopted through behavioural reinforcement and on-the-job mentoring. This can then be heavily enhanced/ changed by the informal message, which is that the new management team will be selected for their abilities to live these behaviours – in effect they will then be the mentors – and the whole cultural change process will be speeded up. By implication, those current managers who have not lived these values and behaviours should seriously consider their futures.

Question: Should you inform those running recruitment/promotion exercises that some candidates are on the influencers list and some are not?

Answer: In theory, the answer is 'no'. The communications work done previously to encourage positive individuals to apply for relevant management positions should meet your purposes by ensuring that the maximum number of positive influencers with management potential are objectively considered. This work should also have significantly reduced the number of change-negative individuals applying.

In reality, however, the answer is often 'yes' since positive influence will be an important selection criteria for many positions. Also, it is likely that some key individuals running the selection process will be so closely involved with your work that they will be kept informed as part of the strong networking/confidence-building that needs to be done anyway. Typically, these individuals might be the HR director and the head of a change programme.

Question: How do you accurately identify informal networks?

Answer: The best way is first to accurately identify change-positive and open-minded influencers at all levels across an organization and then use them as 'guides' to informal networks. Informal networks are then analyzed through selected respondents and questionnaires that focus on particular network areas, ranging from relevant communications, through information access and specialist knowledge transfer, to process and people problems. These influencers guide the entire process. They work with selected managers to focus questionnaires on relevant networks, advise on reliable participant samples at local levels, analyze and evaluate the results, and help drive forward both follow-up problem analyses and necessary changes.

Question: How do you solve the 'highly connected individual who becomes a bottleneck' problem?

Answer: You talk to these people to find out what information they have, what decisions they're making, that others go to them for. You try to make information accessible elsewhere and change decision-making rights so that colleagues can operate around them. You do things to take those people out of the bottleneck position. As people rise in the organization, they move towards the edge of informal networks. Formally or informally, they should do things that decrease other people's reliance on them. Sometimes they require a little help.

General questions on informal networks

Question: Are people surprised by the power and spread of informal networks?

Answer: No, but they are surprised by who is and who isn't influential across networks. Most people know intuitively that better-connected people tend to be more successful and do better in their careers. But when informal network diagrams are shown to senior managers, they usually can – in advance – identify only a fifth or less of what is really happening. There are always major surprises, about people who are more influential than they thought and people who are much more isolated than expected.

What is often a surprise is when networks of people are identified who agree that they should be working together on the delivery of important developments, but who currently are not. These networks may be very extensive. This is, however, good news, since once identified, there is little to stop people getting on with changing and developing whatever is needed, and that is the whole point of the exercise.

Question: What sorts of people tend to be more or less influential than executives expect?

Answer: It's surprisingly common to find that 'high fliers' who come to senior management attention are not influential with many of their colleagues. They are more politically aware, and executives expect them to be at the centre of informal networks. Frequently, however, they show up on the edges of these networks.

Similarly, managers and others who have recently been recruited into an organization because of their good track records show up poorly in networks. They have to prove themselves before they become influential and this often takes at least 6 months.

In contrast, quite junior employees who do their work well, have strong social contacts with work colleagues and have been with the organization for 5 years or more tend to dominate the influence networks. There is generally more real attention paid to peoples' knowledge and skill informally than in the formal setting. In the latter, sadly, it is status and formal power that tend to dominate.

Question: What do you look for in a typical informal network?

Answer: It depends on the type of network. In 'broad' networks (such as communications, knowledge sharing, collaboration, and so on) you look for certain key patterns. Who are highly connected, who are 'brokers' between different organizational areas and who are relatively isolated on the edges of informal networks? The people who are highly connected, either because of their jobs or because they are accessible and valued by colleagues, may inadvertently become overloaded. They are then in danger of holding up the work of others. They may become bottlenecks. Discovering both the potential for bottlenecks and the causes of them is critical. The first is about knowing; the second is about being able to dismantle or work around the bottlenecks.

Also, people who play dominant, positive roles in an informal network can seriously disrupt organizations when they retire, get promoted or move to a different organization.

In contrast, relatively isolated individuals on the edges of networks may be under-performing and need help, or they may be highly focused specialists who need a certain amount of isolation to perform at their best.

Only by using local, relevant influencers in network evaluation workshops can the underlying issues become clear. It is very easy (and usually flawed) for managers and consultants to make assumptions on underlying problems. Their main roles in these workshops should be to probe - and to listen. As ever, discovery and 'finding out' is the key.

Question: Why are some people poorly connected?

Answer: Some of them are genuine under-performers who lack ability or motivation. Some are concentrating on the nine-to-five job and are not engaged with the organization – making very little discretionary effort. Some are relatively isolated, not from choice but because of poor recruitment or poor induction into the business. Some specialists need quite a lot of isolation to work at their best. Some are just very new to their jobs.

When evaluating what to do about isolated people it is best to adopt an open mind and a 'horses for courses' approach.

Question: Many organizations have tried collaboration tools. How well do they work?

Answer: The only consistently useful medium for collaboration across sites or countries is instant messaging. That's pretty harsh and of course there are exceptions. No database today is as effective as a human being for the kind of information people need, particularly where innovation is concerned. Instant messaging comes closest to replicating the iterative conversations that take place around coffee machines and lunch tables.

Question: How effective are team-building exercises in building collaboration?

Answer: Team building can be useful to a degree in building collaboration. Often, however, these exercises are not effective in creating an awareness of 'who knows what' across an organization. Unless you carry out ONA scans to assemble networks of skills, knowledge and expertise, you are often working in the dark. Almost universally, after a merger or a large-scale change implementation, there are plans for intergroup collaboration. But, in practice, collaboration is limited – mainly because people don't know 'who knows what'.

There is, moreover, an underlying problem with conventional team building models. The vast majority of employees would rather work in effective teams than in groups practising internecine warfare. So why does it not happen automatically? While there are skills needed for team leaders and their colleagues in the team, often it is the cultural norms of the organization that inhibit team working. In this case, the better the team building exercise, the more problems it will create. Expectations become high – to be dashed against the rocks of a disabling culture.

Question: Do you also look for people who should collaborate but don't?

Answer: Yes, you should always look for potentially inhibiting 'disconnects'. There are always situations where employees should be communicating in specific ways, but it is just not happening. Hierarchy, culture differences, language and physical remoteness are all possible causes of 'disconnects'. But you need to ask the right questions of the right people to get a clear picture. This is where the ubiquitous change-positive influencers and selective, probing ONA questions come into their own.

Question: Can informal networks really be managed?

Answer: Yes, but there are limits. ONA scans will provide crucial insights, as described throughout this book. The trend towards knowledge work in de-layered organizations will increasingly depend on balanced formal and informal networks for the effective delivery of products and services. But always remember the golden rule:

> *'Never forget that you are dealing with informal personal networks, where individuals ultimately decide what they personally will agree to do.'*

It all depends on what you mean by that word 'managed'. If the mental model is command and control, the answer is a resolute NO. If the mental model is about manager as facilitator and coach, then the answer shifts to a YES.

Question: How sophisticated can network tools get and still be useful?

Answer: There is still scope for increased sophistication in network analysis tools, although some of the leading products are approaching 'awesome' today. The key boundary on sophistication is that the software is useful as long as it *assists* human interpretation and analysis – taking away much of the analysis effort. Beyond that, however, there are real constraints. Once software tries to replace relevant human insight, many dangers lurk!

Appendix 2:
Final Reflections on
'Leadership and Change'

The use of selected influencers and informal networks in running successful modern businesses represents a profound change for most organizations. Many readers of this book will seek to reconcile or contrast the ideas here with those presented in other books and presentations that they have perused over the years.

In this last section, therefore, many of the business management ideas that have received widespread publicity are debated from an informal networks perspective. Selected ideas mentioned briefly in the main body of the book are expanded and discussed in more detail. Some of the underlying logic of the approach is debated. Ideas from some of the leading management thinkers are hotly contested, while others are warmly applauded. Readers are invited to reflect on their own experiences and views.

Leadership

There is much confusion about the term 'leadership' that has grown up over recent years. As a generality, it is treated as if it is different from 'management'. Exploring the reasons for this will help to throw some light on why leadership failures are so common, and how to change the mental model to one with a higher probability of success.

A commonly used definition of the difference is that of Warren Bennis: 'Leaders are people who do the right thing; managers are people who do things right.' Warren Bennis has several other words to say on this subject. For example:

- 'failing organizations are usually over-managed and under-led';

- 'good leaders make people feel that they're at the very heart of things, not at the periphery';

- 'leaders keep their eyes on the horizon, not just on the bottom line';

- 'leadership is the wise use of power. Power is the capacity to translate intention into reality and sustain it';

- 'the manager accepts the status quo; the leader challenges it';

- 'the manager asks how and when; the leader asks what and why';

- 'the manager has a short-range view; the leader has a long-range perspective'.

Superficially, these ideas may be seductive, but there are three things wrong with the very idea of there being a difference between leaders and managers.

The first is that 'leadership' sounds much more glamorous than 'management'. This fits nicely with the idea of the charismatic, high-profile, media-exposure-hungry CEO – who appears in front of video cameras at every available opportunity. There is a minor detail that such people often miss when focusing on 'doing the right thing' – that is the need to do the right thing with a degree of competence, so that the end result is positive added value, and not just another misconceived leap into the unknown. This is another way of saying that management skills are still needed. The 'right thing' has to be done 'right'.

The second is that there is an unspoken assumption that 'leadership' is for the few, and that means top management in the organization. In fact, successful teams are like successful organizations – leaders are found throughout, in many different roles and many different reporting relationships – including those that do not involve the CEO.

The third is that as soon as the skills required for success in management are studied, and compared with those required for success in leadership, the two sets turn out to be identical, providing only that two further, very reasonable, assumptions are made:

- Managers have to produce their results in the longer term, as well as the short term.

- Leaders have to produce results, as well as visions of the future.

This is an important point, since it means that any separation of the development of the skills for management and leadership is only likely to produce very poor results. Incompetent visionaries mixed with bean counters masquerading as managers is not a recipe for success in any business.

In fact, the debate continues with three other things that Warren Bennis said:

- 'Leadership is the capacity to translate vision into reality.'

- 'The most dangerous leadership myth is that leaders are born – that there is a genetic factor to leadership. This myth asserts that people simply either have certain charismatic qualities or not. That's nonsense; in fact, the opposite is true. Leaders are made rather than born.'

- 'Taking charge of your own learning is a part of taking charge of your life, which is the sine qua non in becoming an integrated person.'

The first implies that there is a set of knowledge and skills that is required beyond the ability to devise and articulate a vision.

The second, and particularly the emphasis of the word 'made', means that there is an act of intentionality required, the end result of which is the acquisition of the knowledge and skills required for success in leadership.

Finally, the third observation contains the logical 'crunch'. Learning is about acquiring knowledge and skill. It is not about becoming charismatic, or any other aspect of the persona. We are what we are, and no learning process can change that. All we can do is to study what successful leaders and managers actually do, and try to adopt patterns of behaviour that match the research success patterns.

Which takes us back to the point made above. The knowledge and skills required for success in management (with a longer term perspective) are exactly the same as those required for leadership (with a focus on delivering actual results). In other words, leaders need to be good managers as well; managers need to be good leaders as well. Missing part of this equation in either direction simply results in slightly different kinds of failure.

Various other pieces of research over the years have confirmed this point again and again. Some insights that demonstrate this have been summarized below:

'Nowhere is the test of social skill in management practice better in evidence than in the leadership of men through change.'

> *'It would, in fact, not be untrue to say that change is an inevitable corollary of progressive management and perhaps even its symbol.'*

> Source: E F L Brech – The principles and practice of management

This was written in 1953! Quite apart from the use of both 'management' and 'leadership' in the same sentence, there is a bit of a challenge to the idea that managing change is new. Interestingly enough, Brech sees managing change as requiring the application of social skills. He goes on to quote Elton Mayo as saying that social skills require:

> *'... the capacity to receive communications from others and to respond to the attitudes and ideas of others in such fashion as to promote congenial participation in a common task.'*

It must be pointed out that the last requires much finding out and listening, which is a long way away from the idea of the charismatic leader who thinks it is sufficient to dream up a vision, and obsessively communicate to others the need to follow the lead. This is the exhortation route that is just another manifestation of the good old command and control style of management or leadership, which has been researched to death, and proven not to work – even in the short term.

For the rest of these reflections, the terms management and leadership are treated as interchangeable.

Change programmes versus change processes and change management

Change programmes have a very poor track record of success. In essence, there are three main types of change programme, when classified by the nature of what made it necessary to have a change programme. The first is that of an external change, be it regulatory, market-driven involving competitor activity, or social change including changes in buying fashions. The second occurs when the organization gets into some sort of crisis, frequently driving the need to reduce costs. The third is when a new 'management fad or fashion' appears.

The last of these is a special case, and is dealt with first, as there is often little rationality to the decision to make the change. Much research has been done on management fads and fashions: the information quoted here is taken from *Fuzzy Management,* by Keith Grint (1997). Keith Grint quotes the work of

Pascale, who in 1990 assembled a list of management changes in practices over a 40-year period. The list includes:

Decision trees	Managerial grid	Satisfiers/ dissatisfiers	Theory X and Theory Y	Brainstorming
T-group training	Theory Z	Conglomeration	Management by objectives	Decentralization
Diversification	Experience curve	Strategic business units	Zero base budgeting	Value chain
Wellness	Quality circles/TQM	Excellence	Restructuring/ delayering	Portfolio management
Management by walking about	Matrix management	Just-in-time/ Kanban	Intrapreneuring	Corporate culture
One minute manager	Globalization	Cycle time/ speed	Visioning	Workout
Empowerment	Continuous improvement	Learning organization	Business process re-engineering	Transformation

There are some changes in management practices missing from the list above, including:

Balanced score card	Intuition	Leadership	Competency frameworks	Outsourcing
Knowledge management	KPIs	Innovation	Performance management	Corporate governance

A quick piece of arithmetic concludes that there is a new management fashion, on average, every year. What are top managers to make of this? If there is sense in all of these ideas – they are all of great practical value, as distinct from being mere fashions – then every year management must introduce another change. Given that none of these changes can produce anything serious by way of real improvement in results in much less than 2 years, the implication is that the organization will be in a state rather like a dog chasing its tail – with about the same result!

Given that the various changes listed above also have a short half-life – like flared trousers they go out of fashion almost as fast as they come into it – probably about 2 to 3 years, there is little evidence to suggest that change programmes designed to introduce such changes will ever have much practical benefit to the organization.

Turning to the first two classes, a similar comment is appropriate for both. Both represent examples of what so often becomes a wrenching, cataclysmic change, imposed from above, and where there are losers amongst employees. In both cases, the organization has almost certainly failed to respond early enough, fast enough and boldly enough to incoming signals for change.

Which is another way of saying that the need for such change programmes signals an earlier failure of management. Please note that these comments apply specifically to change programmes, not change processes. In this context, a change programme is an event that has a defined start point, a defined end point, a specific set of objectives and is generally subject to some sort of project management discipline.

Change processes are quite different, as they exist over time, and involve many people. They are, in fact, a manifestation of the type of change discussed by Brech. They depend on the social skills of managers, and the key dimension is that of listening and learning, more than talking and telling. With this model, change becomes a way of life in the organization, and is the business of all employees – consider Toyota as the classic example. Given that operational employees are 'the sensors at the periphery of the organization', then, as these are the same people who will first pick up signals implying the need for change, it is less likely that the organization will be slow to respond – and thus generate the need for another wrenching, cataclysmic change.

To develop good change processes, however, requires the application of a number of management skills, in addition to those described above as social skills. They include:

Extending employees' time horizons	Developing customer responsiveness	Seeking ideas	Stimulating ideas	Developing risk tolerance
Communicating consequences	Defining strategic direction (not long-range plans)	Building a future orientation	Creating market/external orientation	Enabling emergence

Jim Collins – 'Good to Great'

This book summarizes the outcome of extensive research into how some companies make it from the merely good to become great. The key lessons can be expressed as:

LEVEL FIVE LEADERSHIP

No high-profile leaders, no media hungry leaders in the 'heroic leader' model. What is needed is a blend of personal humility and professional will. They never lose sight of the objective and focus on building an organizational organism that will outlast them – and outperform the market place when they are long gone.

FIRST WHO, THEN WHAT

First get the right people on the bus, and then worry about where to drive it. Good people will help to assess the direction needed and help you get there. With the best strategic ideas in the world, a bus full of non-fare paying passengers is no basis on which to build a great business.

CONFRONT THE BRUTAL FACTS, BUT NEVER LOSE FAITH

This is a version of the Stockdale paradox – the prisoner of war who faced up to the realities of his position, avoided wishful thinking – and survived where many did not. Great businesses are built on a foundation of facing up to their real status in time and space – but never losing faith that, at the end, the organization can and will prevail.

THE HEDGEHOG CONCEPT – SIMPLICITY WITHIN 3 CIRCLES

We have to get beyond mere competence. Just because we are good at something is no basis for building a great company. If there is no basis for being best in the world at your core business, there is no basis for greatness. The three circles are 'what are we passionate about?', 'What could we become best in the world at?' and 'What is the key economic denominator that will enable us to grow our business?'

A CULTURE OF DISCIPLINE

With disciplined thought and action, hierarchy and bureaucracy become redundant. With a culture of discipline, controls are no longer needed. A combination of entrepreneurship and discipline is the basis for great performance.

TECHNOLOGY ACCELERATORS

Technology alone is never the basis for building greatness. Technology dependent companies often drown in their indulgence in the latest and brightest technology. Great companies use selected technologies that have the potential to accelerate their growth.

THE FLYWHEEL AND THE DOOM LOOP

Revolutions, dramatic change programmes and wrenching restructurings just set the scene for the next round of cataclysmic change. What is needed is consistent small pushes at the periphery of the wheel, one turn at a time, until it picks up speed – and then builds up enough momentum to acquire an effective life of its own – minimizing the need for major change programmes.

A moment's reflection will point to the fact that the ideas here encompass both leadership and management in the sense described at the beginning of these reflections, reinforcing the point that, for success, managers need to be good leaders, as leaders need to be good managers.

It should also be noted that the prescription specifically points away from change programmes in the direction of the manager facilitating an ongoing change process. By definition, the change process involves many people.

And now we know how to identify who these people are…

Organization cultures, values and performance

Organization culture is 'funny stuff' – at least to a lot of people. It may be regarded as the sort of 'fluffy, soft and squishy stuff' that is the proper domain of industrial psychologists, but nothing to do with real business managers. To take this position would be to totally misunderstand the true nature of organizational culture. Try this as a working definition:

> *'The customs, ideas and values of a particular civilization, society, social group or organization, especially at a particular point in time.'*

In this definition, culture adds up to an unwritten set of rules that govern the behaviour of members of the group or organization. The culture gives people permission to behave in certain ways and prohibits other types of behaviour. In this way, culture is part of the informal system that operates in all organizations, that governs employee behaviour. Clearly there are other drivers of behaviour, including the organization's formal systems, and the characteristics of individuals themselves. Organization culture is, however, a strong driver of behaviour in itself and managers ignore it at their peril.

Before moving on, it is probably worth underlining the importance of organization culture with one observation. The *only* driver of performance is what employees *do*. It is not what they think, feel or know. These only become important when they become drivers of behaviour. Necessarily, this includes all managers as well as operational employees. It is what managers *do* to design organizations, their structures and processes. It is what customer-facing employees *do* that customers observe and react to.

It is what managers *do* that employees interpret, to make meaning out of the messages received, much more than just the spoken word. Problems start to emerge when there is a contradiction between what managers say and their other actions. The old adage 'do what I say, not what I do' does not work with managers' behaviour in organizations, if consistent behaviour that adds value to the organization, its customers and employees is the aim.

This point illustrates a key lesson about organizational culture, and that is the conflict that occurs in employees' minds when there is a difference between an organization's espoused values and the real values received through informal messages. It is this conflict that is one source of stress at work. Other consequences are frustration, alienation and what is sometime labelled as 'malicious obedience'.

To explain this more fully, we turn to the topic of 'organizational permissions'.

First, please note that formal statements of espoused values include video messages; posters on the wall; e-mailed bulletins, newsletters; briefing sessions; communication meetings; and management messages on notice boards. However much management might try, obsessively or otherwise, to communicate their messages about the values and behaviour employees are expected to display, these messages are occasional.

The informal messages that contain often contradictory messages are, by contrast, frequent and unending. These are 'organizational permissions'. There are three sources, namely the design of organizational structures; the design of organizational processes; and the behaviour of senior managers.

An example helps to illustrate the point:

> *A very large fleet rental company had made the decision to take over responsibility for the residual value of its rental vehicles, at the end of*

the 3-year lease period. When someone realized that the condition of the returned vehicle might be such that the underwritten value would not be achieved, it was decided to modify the changeover process. Old cars being brought back had to be handed in by 10:00 and the new car would not be available for collection until after 14:00 the following (working) day. In the meantime, the vehicle condition could be checked and a customer invoice for repairs issued if necessary. The fleet was such that there were over 500 vehicle changeovers, every day of the working week, including Fridays.

At about the same time the CEO decided that increased customer focus was an essential for the business to stay competitive, so he made a video, exhorting all employees on why they needed to be more customer focused. He insisted that all employees should watch the video. In the employees' perception, this just acted as a break within their working day of telling another customer that '... they could not have their new car until tomorrow ...'. The real message was explicitly clear – the company's bottom line was much more important than its customers.

This is a good example of a general principle, when it is noticed, that most changeover transactions involved multiple interactions between the company, its dealers and customers. This meant that there were literally thousands of daily events when the customers' needs got kicked into touch. There were almost as many occasions when call centre staff were heard to express their position as, 'I would really like to help you, but the rules won't allow me to.'

In this ocean of informal messages about taking care of the bottom line, at the cost of customer service, the CEO's video message was either just 'noise on the line', or, worse, a source of real anger and frustration. Not surprisingly, the turnover of staff in the call centre was high.

The first key message in all of this is that organizational culture counts. The second is that you cannot change it by exhortation. Try that route, and there are more likely to be negative effects than positive outcomes. There are two possible ways of approaching the challenge of organizational culture and values: one works and the other does not.

The failure route is to decide what the culture and/or values of the organization need to be, do the design work, plan the initiative – and then go and tell people what they are. These formal messages simply drown in the mass of contradictory, informal messages that hit employees, day in and day out – the 'permissions'.

Organizational culture and values can only be discovered – it is possible to find out what they are. This requires managers to get out of their offices, and go listen to influencers and other employees. It requires a genuinely enquiring frame of mind, and good questioning and listening skills. It requires managers to accept negative feedback when it occurs – which it will. The very act of such a 'finding out' exercise will, in itself, have a positive effect, with just one caveat. The lessons learned must be translated into observable changes; otherwise one more round of cynicism will set in, focused on the gap between what managers say and what they do.

Once the real culture and values have been discovered, there are only two possibilities. Either all is well or it is not. In the former case, all managers need to do is to congratulate themselves, and repeat the 'finding out' exercise at frequent intervals, to ensure that nothing is changing. In the latter case, another 'finding out' exercise is required. This must be designed to review all the formal structures and processes, plus management and influencer behaviour, that are the source of informal organizational permissions, and change all and every one that contain messages driving negative aspects of organizational culture and values. Sometimes this is just a matter of changing established procedures – such as performance management criteria. Sometimes it is more difficult, requiring person-to-person reinforcements of 'good' behaviours and challenges to 'bad' behaviours on a day-to-day basis.

This can never be a one-off exercise, since 'drift' in organizations will threaten any positive achievements made. Drift is the set of slow, insidious changes in organizational practices that never seems to work in the favour of organizational health. Somehow, a focus on the long-term growth and health of the organization succumbs to the need to achieve monthly numbers; bureaucratic rules take over from simple principles (values) that enable employees to apply their knowledge, skills and experience in novel ways; a free exchange of information between managers and employees transmutes into one-way-downward diktats.

Still, perseverance will generate its own reward. Developing an organizational culture that supports improved performance and a big pay off to the organization, its customers and employees can only add value to the bottom line anyway.

Influence, influencers and resistance to change

How individuals acquire influence is multi-faceted, although there are common themes. For a start, there are different applications of influence, and these will impact on the mindset that is appropriate, and the skill set that needs to be applied. The most common, and one of the most researched, is that of the sales person. In these days of buying through the Internet, many sales people are account managers, as distinct from 'conquest sales people'.

The difference is generally in the main thrust of their sales effort. For the conquest sales person, the main objective is to open new accounts; for the account manager, the main objective is to maximize revenues from existing accounts. In practice, both types of sales person do both – it is the balance that varies.

The universal truth for both types of 'selling' is about questioning and listening. Influence is gained when one person finds out the overt and hidden needs of the other, and then shows that person a route to dealing with them. 'Telling' has very little to do with selling. Both types of sales people need to be good at planning, although the applications vary again. For the conquest sales person, the main issue is about how to prioritize the various sales opportunities in the territory, and how best to allocate time to developing them. For the account manager, the challenge is how to penetrate what are quite often large organizations, with their own internal influence networks, and build an influence network generally favourable to the sales person's product or service.

Recent research has shown that, in the main, buyers need to gain actual benefit from the sales process as well as the product itself. This means that the sales person has to focus on helping the buyer solve problems, and that reinforces the old idea of the need for consultative selling. It also underlines the need for 'finding out'. This means that the account manager has to find out what is troubling a wide range of people across the buyer's organization, help solve the problems identified, and, through that process, build an influence network. This view is backed by research that people in the formal position of buyers are more concerned about the mechanics of the buying process, and corporate governance issues, than in making the actual choice of supplier and product.

The decision maker is often an executive in the buying organization, and their decisions are hugely influenced by any number of other people – the internal influence network. It is this network that the account manager has to discover; it is the problems of the people in it that have to be found out and solved. Networking and building influence networks are the key skills for account managers – as they are for others.

Interestingly, research in 2006 into what produces success for project managers arrived at a similar conclusion. Project management skills themselves were a bit like delivering quality in a competitive market – it is the essential requirement to play at all. But project management skills are like quality – on their own they do not guarantee success. For project managers, it is their ability to build a supportive network, find out the issues that its members have to resolve – and provide solutions for them through the direction and management of the project.

This leads to a tentative conclusion that good, strategic questioning and listening skills might just be a universal requirement for all people in management roles – and so it turns out to be. (It all depends on the definition of 'managing' that we adopt. The one used here is, 'Managers make things happen through other people.' If that statement is true, then the critical things that managers do must occur when they are face-to-face with other people. That observation leads on to the question of management style.)

SALES PEOPLES' PLANNING SKILLS ARE NOT ALWAYS TOP NOTCH!

A consultant was out with a sales person one day, when, during a stop for coffee he decided to pursue the topic of planning. 'Tell me, Harry, How do you plan your sales call activities?' he asked. 'I don't understand the question,' said the salesman. 'How do plan the attack on your territory?" was the follow-up question. Harry said, 'I am still not quite sure what you are driving at?' 'Well, how do you decide which way to drive, when you leave your house in the morning?' – the consultant thought a simple version of the question might get through, and it did.

'Now I've got it – well it all depends,' said Harry. 'On what?' 'Well, it all depends on which pub I went to the night before.' The sharp intake of breath indicated to Harry quite clearly that more was needed, without additional questioning. 'You see, in the village where I live, the lane in front of my cottage is very narrow, and I can't turn the car round. If I went to the Pig and Whistle, it's pointing north, and if it was the Dun Cow, the car points south. So, if it was the Dun Cow, I do South Oxfordshire, and if not, I do the North.'

Negotiating

Another topic that has been very well researched, that is closely related to influencing, is that of negotiating. The similarity is indicated thus:

- *Influencing* – gaining commitment to actions by another party to meet pre-determined objectives.

- *Negotiating* – Gaining mutual commitment to actions by two or more parties so that all parties meet their predetermined priority objectives.

The reason for introducing the negotiating concept here is that power is at the heart of all negotiating and power is important for influencing as well. There are three keys about the application of power in negotiating that are also important for influencing. The first is that, because of the definition offered above, power cannot be used to override the interests of other people. 'Commitment' does not include malicious obedience! Essentially, anything the other parties do must enable them to meet their own objectives.

The second is that there are several sources of power, of which only one is the skill set of the influencer, as suggested above. The prime power sources are:

LEGITIMACY

Legitimacy is acquired through a number of aspects of the involved parties or their actions, many of which are more symbolic than real. An individual's qualifications or experience is one source of legitimacy. Another is the printing of policies and procedures, or price lists.

COMMITMENT

This is partly about preparation and analysis, before the event – see below under time and effort. It is also about belief in the outcomes that are possible, and the willingness to twist and turn in a thinking process that is heavily focused more on finding ways and means, especially in respect of increasing actual or perceived power, than on lamenting the difficulties that might exist, imagined or real.

RISK TAKING

There are no risk-free actions available to anyone, in any sphere of managing that involves people, money, resources or time. There are no guaranteed outcomes to any negotiating ploy or position. Each contains the potential of advantage, and each equally contains the possibility of failure. A good example is the use of constructive deadlock – it may unblock the blockage to getting the deal, or it may lose the deal totally! An assessment of the risks that are acceptable and those which may be acceptable to the other party can often produce considerable power and advantage.

TIME AND EFFORT

This is primarily about the amount of time spent in preparation and the willingness to commit more time to the actual process of negotiation, plus acceptance that it may be a multi-stage process. The rule of thumb for preparation is a 2.5 to 1 rule – allow at least two and a half times as much time for preparation as that which is expected to be needed for the negotiating meetings themselves.

KNOWLEDGE

In this context, knowledge refers mainly to knowledge of the subject. It is the ability to pose questions that the other party might be unable to answer, and the ability to answer their questions and points based on sound technical knowledge. Knowledge also implies the ability to be more creative in the development of negotiating options – research shows that skilled negotiators use nearly four times as many options per topic as average negotiators.

MONEY

Money is the universal lubricant that enables parties to the negotiation to get things done. The possession of it in greater quantities than the other party also implies the ability to accept more risk – with possibly greater terminal damage.

SKILLS

The key skill here is that of negotiating itself. There are observable differences in the methods and behaviours used by skilled negotiators compared with the averagely successful negotiator, and they can and should be learned. Again and again the skilled negotiator concludes a more favourable deal than the less skilled competition.

RELATIONSHIPS AND NETWORKS

This is partly the power that is inherent in a majority position, and again this may be more perceived than real, but it is power nonetheless. Importantly, it is also access to the knowledge, skills and resources of other members of the network that can be brought to play in the negotiation. A final component is that of critical mass – if the perceived weight of the influence group that has to be 'moved' is sufficiently great, many negotiators will downrate their perceived chances of success, and their power along with them.

This leads to the third key. The research on power in relation to negotiating produces an interesting result. Put a group of sales people in a room and ask them who has the power when negotiating with buyers and mostly they conclude that it is the buyer. Put a group of buyers into a room and ask them who has the power when negotiating with sales people and mostly they conclude that it is the sales person. Since neither group is right, this leads to the observation that it is common for people to assign themselves less power than they actually have, and more power to the other party than they actually have.

When the two (sales and buyer) groups are put together, generally they fail to agree on who has the power. They discuss a simple truth table, that has four options – sales people have the power; buyers have the power; both have the power; neither has the power. In practice all these options are wrong. The right answer to the question 'Who has the power?' is that power is held by the party that believes they have it, irrespective of formal role. Power is more about a perception of power than any formal assignation of authority.

This leads us to the conclusion that successful influencers and negotiators think long and hard about their sources of power and work hard to maximize them. (Successful negotiators also think long and hard about the other party's sources of power and how they can either diminish it or at least diminish the perception of it). As power is all about perception, good influencers thus increase their confidence that they have power, and thus their confidence in handling their interactions with other people.

A moment's reflection will point to the insight that here is yet another example of the critical need for managers, influencers and negotiators – and most managers are in all three roles most of the time – to be good at 'finding out'. This arises both from the definitions of influencing and negotiating, and from the actual behaviour of people acting in those roles.

Management style

The problem with this topic is that it is another multi-faceted topic, but often treated as if it is simple. It is not.

For a start, there is much confusion about the terms autocracy and democracy. Except in extreme and very rare circumstances, neither has any place in management – if they are practised as consistent styles. As difficult is any assumption that, on the one hand, command and control styles of management are 'bad', as participative styles of management are 'good'. Neither is a universal truth; both have their parts to play. Consider the following:

It was noted above that the critical things that managers do occur when they come face to face with other people. Analysis of the interactive behaviours of managers shows two, distinct successful styles of management conversation profiles. These are related to the traditional autocratic/democratic styles of management behaviour but are not identical to them. According to the continuum that emerged, the range of styles is depicted below. The styles relate to how managers get their decisions implemented.

Tells   The manager gives an instruction, with no explanation about the purpose of, reason for it or objective that is being pursued. HOW to do the job is included in the instruction.

Sells   The issue of the instruction is preceded by an explanation of the purpose of, reason for it or objective that is being pursued. The HOW is still included.

Tests   After an explanation of the purpose of the decision to be made, reason for it or the objective to be achieved, the manager offers a suggestion on HOW the job could be done, and asks for the employee's reactions - do they agree YES or NO? ('Tests' is generally used in a one-to-one conversation).

The employee may feel that the manager's think bubble contains the message, 'It's only a suggestion, but don't forget who's making it' and may rush to agree. The manager retains the right to decide on the HOW.

Managing Styles

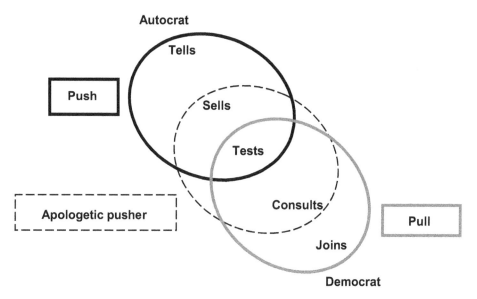

Figure A2.1   Comparison of a spectrum of managing styles

Consults This is similar to TESTS, but after the initial explanation, the manager offers no suggestion on the HOW. Instead, employees are asked to offer their suggestions on HOW the job might be done. The manager retains the right to decide the HOW. ('Consults' is generally used in a conversation with a group).

Joins At this level, the manager gives up the right to decide, and the decision is made by the group, of which the manager may or may not be a member.

Both of the extreme styles Autocrat (tells) and Democrat (joins) are poor motivators: in the first case because of the resistance that is brought about by the autocrat and in the second case because managers have abdicated their responsibility to decide. The two successful styles are labeled PUSH and PULL. PUSH encompasses 'Tells', 'Sells' and 'Tests', and is, therefore, nearer to Autocrat, but not so extreme, and PULL encompasses 'Tests', 'Consults' and 'Joins', and is, therefore, nearer to Democrat, but again, not so extreme.

In passing, there is one other managing style that was identified – the 'Apologetic Pusher'. This is the person who has read something, somewhere, about the need for participation, but also that managers need to be 'dynamic decision makers'. In an attempt to reconcile these two conflicting demands, at the same time, the Apologetic Pusher wobbles about uncertainly between the two extremes – and uses the most unsuccessful managing style of all. The problem is the extreme uncertainty caused – is this manager pushing or pulling, – coming or going? Most people would rather work for an autocrat – at least there is clarity in the style, even if it is an unfortunate one.

Further research has shown that there is a time/result relationship appropriate to these management styles which is depicted in Figure A2.2.

The graph shows push style as being favorable when fast results are required and risks are low. Risk, in this context, is that concerned with rejection of the manager's approach, because there is no perception of the need for a high-pressure approach – as there would be if, for example, a very real crisis was at hand.

Where similar risks are high and delays can be tolerated in producing results, pull style is preferred. This will especially be true when the need is for the manager and team to be aiming for long-term growth.

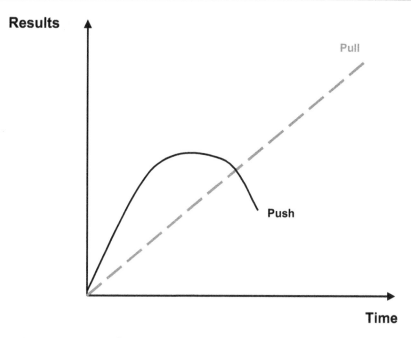

Figure A2.2   Impact of pull and push approaches over time

The manager who will be most successful will be the one who recognizes the demands of the situation in terms of time constraints, risks and the need for commitment, and who selects the appropriate management/decision-making style. Where a manager predominantly uses pull style, the occasional use of push, especially where there is a perceived crisis on hand and time is limited, will have limited risks.

Where a manager has a predominantly push style, and tries occasionally to use pull, the most common response will be one of mistrust and suspicion, rather than a ready willingness to contribute to the decision-making process. In fact, as many managers' natural, unconscious style is experienced as closer to that of autocrat, when an attempt is made to create involvement through applying a pull style after the extensive application of push or beyond, one or both of two things is likely to happen.

The first is that the real style, as perceived by those on the receiving end, will still be closer to autocrat than pull. The second is that the reaction will be one of rejection, along the lines of, 'You manager, me worker – you make the decisions, I implement them – you tell me what you want me to do, and I will (may?) do it. If it all goes pear shaped, that will be down to you – you made the decision.' Malicious obedience is not unknown in these circumstances –

'workers' know they have to obey the boss's instructions, but their commitment may be stronger to proving they were right all along than to helping the boss gets the results wanted.

Many managers are not consciously aware of their conversational behaviour, and their profile tends to be strongly skewed towards push style or beyond – heading towards that of the autocrat. The pull style is strongly dependent on good questioning and listening skills.

According to McKinsey (Managing your organization by the evidence, 2006) there are four top failing management practices. These are:

1. The carrots and sticks of incentives appear to be the least effective of the four options commonly used to motivate and encourage employees to perform well and stay with a company.

2. Applied in isolation, KPIs and similar control mechanisms (such as performance contracts) are among the least satisfactory options for improving accountability.

3. Relying on a detailed strategy and plan is far from the most fruitful way to set a company's direction.

4. Command and control leadership – the still-popular art of telling people what to do and then checking up on them to see that they did it – is among the least effective ways to direct the efforts of an organization's people.

The link between command and control management styles, and that of the autocrat, as defined above, is clear. This means that yet another piece of evidence has been collected, reinforcing much older messages, that autocratic management styles, if applied as the one and only style, simply do not work.

Managing styles and complexity – and informal networks

A relatively new perspective on control styles is provided by Ralph Stacey in *The Chaos Frontier*, 1991; *Complexity and Management*, 2000; and *Complex Responsive Processes in Organizations*, 2001.

Each individual human being is a complex adaptive system. Bring a group of human beings together in an organization and the level of complexity increases hugely.

In most business organizations attempts are made to prescribe relationships between people and their behaviour by defining structures and processes (these are forms of control behaviour by managers). This layer of complexity is generally introduced to try to stop what would otherwise be seen as chaotic behaviour. In reality, a hidden or shadow organization always operates, as people circumvent the formal organization in order to get their jobs done and create new relationships by joining informal networks. Informal networks also increase the degree of complexity in the organization.

It would be possible to regard organizations as merely complicated, as distinct from complex. This would, however, be to misunderstand the nature of what happens in real organizations, as people try to handle the consequences of managers' attempts to direct and control what happens.

Control mechanisms

There are three types of change that happen in organizations – closed, contained and open – each of which exists in the past, the present or the future. When we think about management attempts to exert control, the relationship with the timing of the change can be expressed as:

- trying to control the effects of changes that have already happened;

- trying to control the effects of changes that are happening NOW;

- trying to control the effects of expected future changes.

In all three, the change can be closed, contained or open.

- Closed change operates over short timescales. Business parameters and the variables affecting it are known. Cause and effect are known, and experience is a reliable guide to action. Closed change timescales are getting shorter.

- Contained change operates over longer timescales. Business parameters and the variables affecting it are probabilistic. Cause and effect are only subject to assessment of probability and prediction. Experience is no longer a totally reliable guide to action, but can be used to help assess probability of causes and predict most likely outcomes. Contained change timescales are getting shorter.

- Open change operates over even longer timescales. Business parameters and the variables affecting it are volatile, and probability and prediction break down. Experience no longer has any value in predicting possible outcomes. Possible scenarios become too many and too varied to be handled. It may even be impossible to distinguish between variables that are important and those that are not.

Each type of change demands a different kind of control mechanism. Closed change is traditionally subject to control by variance – we know what should be happening, and why, and how to remedy the effects of the change. Contained change is subject to control by 'grand design' – we know the direction we are intending to go, often of the 'roughly west' variety, and implement actions that we predict will probably take us in the desired direction. Open change only has one form of control that is appropriate, and that is by trial and error. Systemic learning becomes the order of the day.

Managers have a tricky balancing act to perform – every day of the working year. They need to use all three control mechanisms, in each of the three timeframes, often during the same working period. The tensions that can be experienced by managers trying to walk this tightrope can be extreme. Often the manager in question will 'fall off' the tightrope, and commonly regress to control by variance, whether or not this type of control is appropriate.

The more that high pressure to deliver short-term results is coming down the line from above or from stakeholders, the more this regression to traditional control mechanisms is likely to occur.

Where excessive control by variance is exerted, employees faced with the changing realities communicated through contacts with customers, suppliers and other employees will react the way all sensible employees do – they will ignore the formal rule book and try to get the best result for the business that they can. This is the genesis of informal networks.

In passing, it should be noted that informal networks are not static or fixed. The networks themselves are transitory and volatile. They appear and disappear; they form and reform; their membership is a moving target. They represent a form of unstable equilibrium, operating at the edge of chaos, brought about by their own internal control mechanisms. These control mechanisms include natural survival and experiential learning, the latter arising from the goal-seeking nature of all informal networks.

It should also be noted, in passing, that informal networks are a perfect breeding ground for innovation, as cross-functional groupings bring different and sometime conflicting perspectives to bear in organizational problem-solving processes. Given the goal-seeking nature of these networks, it is not surprising that problems and conflicts are often resolved by negotiated actions that are new, in order to satisfy all parties.

Because of the probably high degree of innovation arising from, and the volatile nature of, informal networks, while each network may be pursuing an informal version of control by grand design, there is no way of predicting the global outcomes that will occur through their activities. In other words, the organization will be exhibiting emergence as defined by Stacey; hence the organization is not just complicated, but actually highly complex.

Given the complexity of real organizations, and the transitory nature of informal networks, it can safely be concluded that, yet again, command and control style management is not appropriate. All informal networks are beyond management control, by their very nature. Management attempts to do so are generally of the 'control by variance' type, with an excess focus on short-term issues, with an inevitable negative impact on innovation – which mostly the self-same managers will demand from their people! Sounds like yet another contradictory message on its way to causing more frustration than positive outcome.

As a final footnote on the subject of managing style, one keen observer of the issue recently summarized the shift in style required as being 'from the sage on the stage to the guide on the side'. Which is a very informal way of saying that managers, (for most of the time), need to act in the role of catalyst, facilitator and coach – the very opposite of top-down, management-driven changes.

Resistance to change

There are both old and new thoughts on this topic, and some are briefly visited in this section.

There is a traditional view that it is middle managers that are a common source of resistance to change. The argument goes like this:

It is managers at the top who observe the condition of the business; who study its position in time and space; who think about the future and the strategic issues that demand attention now. Thus, they are often the people who see the need for change, and the need to stimulate it.

First line supervisors are in a state of change anyway. This arises partly as they are in a formative stage of career development and steep learning curves are still being climbed. They are in very close contact with operational events and often with signals coming in from the world outside the organization. Hence, they are also 'in change'.

It is middle managers who have achieved a degree of security, with generally comfortable incomes. It is middle managers who have achieved their success 'doing things the way we do them around here'. These are the people who designed, built and operated the formal processes and practices of the organization. They are, therefore, the people most threatened by top-down-driven management-inspired changes.

This is a special case of the general argument: people resist change that they do not understand or change that threatens some aspect of their working life.

The argument that people naturally resist all change does not stand up to simple observation. Most people seem to relish change – the need, for example, to keep moving home; the need to go 'somewhere different' on holiday; the need to redecorate and refurnish. The list of changes that people inflict on themselves is endless. The key is that the people in question make the decision to change; they select which new road to go down; they are in control – or, at least, that is what they believe.

In organizations, the argument that all people automatically resist all change is even more fallacious. There are several reasons, but two will suffice here. First, the majority of organizations contain high levels of frustration. People find that there are many barriers in the way of them being more successful in their jobs. They do not need persuasion that changes are needed. The problem is that, so often, senior managers are not finding out what the barriers are and doing enough to dismantle them.

Second, the people on the receiving end of the change have no idea what is actually driving it, and have even less input into what is to be done and how to do it. As a generality, more junior people in the organization receive incoming messages signalling the need for change much earlier than top management and are amazed when there is no perceivable reaction from management. Where it all starts to go horribly wrong is when people cannot see a clear, logical link between the situation on the ground, and what management has decided to do. If the message is received that, here we go with 'another cost-cutting reorganization' to compensate for an earlier management failure to keep the business in good shape, then resistance will be entrenched.

Change failures are due to 'people' factors

All of which is another way of saying that healthy change comes from within, and is difficult to impose from without. One common example from recent times may help to illustrate the point.

CRM is another of those great ideas that does not quite seem to work out in practice. Too many companies have invested very large sums of money in large CRM-oriented IT systems, with little to show by way of return on that investment. Sadly, the evidence suggests that somewhere between 55 and 75 per cent of CRM implementations fail to deliver on the business expectations and objectives of the CRM user. CRM tools are rated very poorly for customer satisfaction among executives of medium- and large-sized organizations.

The failures are mainly associated with implementation, not the system being implemented. Part of the problem is the usual one of definition – failure to appreciate the meaning of the language, and its implications, is a recipe for failure before implementation is even contemplated. There appear to be three different meanings attached to the expression CRM. For convenience, these have been labelled them CRM 1, 2 and 3.

CRM 1 – CUSTOMER RELATIONS MEASUREMENT

There are several different models applied, including the NPP concept (Net Promoter Primer), but they all have one thing in common. This is the measurement of customer satisfaction. Generally, there is little analysis for cause – 'we know that we have a problem but not why' – and the reports generated are, therefore, a listing of various symptoms – of success or failure, or generally a mixture of the two.

In fact, benchmarking is a more common tactic than analysis for cause – comparing 'our' scores with those of similar businesses may lead to much navel contemplation, but is unlikely to lead to much improvement. As with most systems that measure symptoms, with or without benchmarking, little management action follows. Knowing about the existence of a problem tells us little about *how* to solve it. Problem resolution needs analysis for cause before any valid action can be taken. Good analytical tools are needed to drive the analysis, and then a serious management commitment to customer service quality (quality as measured in the customers' terms) before any effective developmental action will follow.

In passing, it might be noted that, if the measurement of customer satisfaction uses measures defined by the supplier, without a little 'finding out' first about what the customer perceives as 'quality', then the whole thing is likely to be doomed to a frenetic pursuit of the wrong objectives. There have been too many cases of expensive investments in PRODUCT quality, of the mechanical or electronic variety, that produced zero improvement in customer satisfaction. The reason is commonly because, to the customer, quality is actually more about service and interactions with the supplier's people. In other words, 'quality' is more about the total package, and not just the 'bits and pieces' themselves.

CRM 3 – CUSTOMER RELATIONS MARKETING

(Taken out of sequence to underline a point). This is marketing that is driven by a segmented customer (and prospect) database, with different messages being conveyed according to the segment. Some systems even differentiate the message according to very detailed customer classifications, or, in some cases, for individual customers.

Generally, the databases that are used are large and complex – and expensive. This is an approach that is likely to fail if one or both of two problems remain in the system. The first, as noted above, arises if there is no adequate knowledge of what it is that the customer really needs, in terms of service or product quality, or anything else for that matter. In this case, the messages are likely to be poorly targeted.

The second arises if the level of satisfaction is currently low. In this circumstance, well-targeted messages may actually be less effective than those that are 'off-target'. The contradiction between the (good) marketing message and the real customer experience will soon be spotted, with the predictable negative reaction: 'How can these people offer to deliver what they patently are not?'

The point here is that CRM 1 and CRM 3 will both fail to add real value to the business, unless CRM 2 is in place and working well.

CRM 2 – CUSTOMER RELATIONS MANAGEMENT

This is the outcome of a change process, designed to develop an organization that is focused on creating and sustaining a high level of customer responsiveness. The change process required will be multi-faceted and complex; it will need to cover the development of new skills; the acquisition of new attitudes and values to drive different behaviours; there will need to be new and different structures and processes, with the designs very specifically incorporating the symbols necessary to enable and underpin the shift of focus and values.

In the case of CRM, this level of change may not even be attempted, because there is no perception of need, through lack of understanding of the implications of a successful CRM programme. It may also not be attempted because a successful change can only come about through the active participation of many people, including operational employees, and that participation must necessarily include the opportunity to provide directed and change-oriented feedback on corporate policies and practices – at which point the ego of some senior managers may get in the way – high self-esteem can be a barrier to processing feedback and learning.

The problem is that, whatever the challenges, unless a successful CRM 2 initiative is implemented, CRM 1 is a waste of time and energy and CRM 3 is disabled. Which is another way of saying that the only CRM programmes that truly succeed are those that tackle CRM 1, 2 and 3 as different facets of an integrated change process. And the difficult bit is CRM 2 – it needs good analysis through CRM 1 to drive it, and itself is a critically important enabler of CRM 3. In short, CRM 2 depends on the engagement and support of many employees, and an open and inquiring approach by management – to find out what it is about the organization that inhibits greater customer service and what needs to change, in the real world of customer-facing employees, to make it all happen.

Drift in organizations – or death by a thousand cuts

Very often, change initiatives don't actually encounter active resistance, but they are rather like old soldiers – they just fade away. This is one example of a more general problem, called drift. As a route into the topic, consider the following very simple model of managing behaviour.

MAINTENANCE VERSUS DEVELOPMENT

Maintenance activities are:

- repeated, cyclical;
- go on day by day, week by week, month by month;
- never finished;
- important for maintaining standards of performance in the business.

Development activities:

- are once-off tasks or projects;

- occupy a finite space in time;

- when finished, are over and done with, never to be repeated;

- are important for developing and improving standards of performance in the business.

A business that achieves a position in which 100 per cent of the energy of the management team is devoted to maintenance activities will fall behind others in the same industry, which are themselves changing and developing. The business is likely first to become static, then to slide gently into decline and ultimately go under.

Although less likely and quite difficult to imagine, a business that achieves a position in which 100 per cent of the energy of the management team is devoted to development activities will send a clear message to employees in the firm that little counts in terms of current performance. Standards will be difficult to maintain and the business is likely to decline very rapidly, and then go under.

This is another way of saying that both types of activities are important, and that keeping a good balance between them is essential. If the balance swings too far in either direction, and becomes extreme, the only real difference in the effect is in the speed with which the business goes under. It is important, however, to recognize that there are also differences between the maintenance/ development balances which are appropriate for different types of job.

For employees in strictly operational jobs – such as routine building cleaning – an appropriate balance will be something like 95:5 in favour of maintenance. For the chairman of the board, the balance will be appropriate when it is something like 95:5 in favour of development. In other words, the balance should swing progressively from maintenance towards development the nearer you get to policy and strategy definition.

Observation of many organizations suggests, however, that this ideal state is rarely achieved in practice. The balance is normally distorted towards maintenance and in only the rarest of examples in the other direction. The reasons for this are complex and compound, and largely about the nature of the formal and informal systems that operate within many organizations, and the symbolic messages that their design contain. A few examples will illustrate:

- The instinct that drives people towards activities that produce high-visibility, short-term results. Most people get satisfaction from achievement and recognition, and may believe that there is little to be gained from the achievement of longer-term developmental goals, which may be difficult to measure, have low visibility anyway and in the interim, totally lack recognition.

- A degree of risk aversion. Maintenance activities generally come into the class of the 'well known' – they have been done many times before. The probability of success is high. Development activities are all a leap into the unknown and there is the probability of failure to be handled.

- Organization information systems mostly add visibility into the area of maintenance results – and information systems are reward systems anyway. That which gets measured gets delivered and that which gets measured and rewarded gets delivered even more. This effect reinforces the instinct that most people have anyway, as noted above.

- Performance management, appraisal and assessment systems that add visibility into the area of maintenance results

- Questions asked excessively by the MD or CEO about maintenance results – 'What was produced/delivered last month/week/ yesterday' – not balanced by developmental questions – 'What are we doing today to enhance future results, customer satisfaction, the motivation and commitment of people, and the general health and vitality of the organization?'. Maintenance-oriented questions distort the message about what is important in the organization (or perhaps state what is actually important more clearly, than all the formal communications systems!)

- The reason for introducing the maintenance/development model is that all change programmes are, by definition, a form of development. (Excluded are those organizations where change is a way of life, or where change is regarded as an unending process. In these cases, it sounds as if the maintenance/development balance is there or thereabouts!)

- Because of the system effects noted in the bullet points above, the natural decay in the maintenance/development balance will always be towards maintenance. In this sense, change programmes – the beasts with a defined start and finish point – are always at risk. This is one example of the widespread phenomenon know as drift. The table below provides a number of other examples of organizational drift:

Desired state	State after drift has occurred
Appropriate balance of maintenance and development activities – balance of short-term performance standards with longer-term goals.	Excessive focus on short-term standards – wheel-spin – fire-fighting – organization in stasis.
Short list of key performance indicators, balanced across internal/external; financial/non-financial; mechanical/people related. All supported by diagnostic information for ad hoc analysis of cause. Exception reporting used.	Long list of performance indicators, mainly inward focused/financial/short term/cyclical. Frequent conflicts between performance indicators. Regular reports and reviews.
Simple principles are used to guide behaviour – support for emergent, complex adaptive strategies and innovation.	There are complex, prescriptive rules that severely limit freedom of decision about responses to a variable environment. Innovation is suppressed.
Performance management models that are output-results focused; use informal, two-way feedback processes; run to variable timings; reporting limited. Same model applies to all employees. A normal and natural part of daily work life.	Employee assessment focused on the person not output results. Regular, formal, one-way downward assessments that focus on skills or competencies. Complex, detailed reporting. Different models for senior people – or not used at all. Regulated and may use artificial constructs such as 3600 feedback.
Strategy is largely emergent, with ad hoc opportunistic decisions used to capitalize on changed conditions or to respond to environmental issues, The power to influence strategy is widely dispersed.	Strategic planning done by senior people or specialists. Decision power held closely to the centre. Long-range plans are used, with annual updates, tied to the budget round. Mostly, strategic plans are long-range financial forecasts.
The organization is flat, and line managers are generalists – they perform their own support functions. Head office/central functions are small. Power is widely distributed.	The organization is deep, and there are many specialist functions. Head office/central functions are large. Most power is retained in the centre.
Budgets are treated as what they are – forecasts, and subject to the standard rule for all forecasts – 'If they are accurate within 5 per cent they were either lucky or wrong'. Small variances are ignored. Trends are more important than monthly figures.	Budgets are treated as sacrosanct. Monthly figures must be met. All variances are treated as serious issues and subject to detailed analysis and reporting – commonly with assignment of blame.
Decisions about the disposal and application of resources are for line managers to make. Budget holders can swap resources between budget heads and share them with other budget holders.	All variations from budgeted allocations of resources have to be approved by the centre. Decisions about resources are held within vertical silos.

Decision processes are fast, objective, frequently cross-functional and focused on achieving high standards of product and customer service quality. Generally, decisions are taken by the people who have to implement them.	Decision processes are slow and rule bound. Conformance is more important than performance. Decisions are often taken within organizational silos and by people who do not have to implement them.
Employees are engaged with the organization to a high degree. Motivation is extrinsic more than intrinsic and stems from the way that employees are managed by their immediate supervisor. Levels of 'flow' are high.	Employees are disengaged from the organization. Motivation is more intrinsic than extrinsic, and the organization relies on a variety of financial and other rewards to motivate employees.

Desired state	State after drift has occurred
'Communications' is something that comes naturally and is part of the normal process of managers and employees getting their jobs done. No topics are off the table. 'Communications' are the responsibility of everyone in the organization.	'Communications' is a formal process and is something that is designed to transmit specific information selectively from the organization to employees. 'Communications' are the responsibility of a specialized department or individual.
Change is a way of life for everyone in the organization. It arises from a non-ending search for ways of improving product and customer service quality – and the effectiveness of the organization in delivering them.	Change is the focus of formal programmes in the organization, with most change being stimulated by top management. Most change is a response to needs imposed from without or above.
Knowledge and skill rate higher than status.	Status rates higher than knowledge and skill.
Interactions within functions and across functional boundaries are characterized by open dialogue. Agreements are negotiated between peers.	Interactions are characterized by hidden agendas and political objectives. Power brokers and influence networks dominate decision making.

Any example of drift from the list above will threaten any major change initiative. This requires continuing management vigilance. But if such a tactic is to be applied, consistently, this begs the question of why a change programme is needed in the first place. Such an approach to management would inevitably mean that a reasonable maintenance/development balance is in place, together with all the other 'desired states' listed in the left-hand column of the table.

In which case, it might be an idea to engage with all the key influencers in informal networks, find out what is the current state of drift in the organization and agree actions to reverse the drift. Now that sounds like a change process well worth pursuing.

Bibliography

Baldock, Robert. *The Last Days of the Giants?*, John Wiley, 2000.

Beer, Stafford. *Designing Freedom*, John Wiley, 1974.

Brech, EFL. *The Principles and Practice of Management*, Longmans, 1963.

Champy, James and Nohria, Nitia. *Fast Forward*, Harvard Business School Publishing, 1996.

Collins, Jim. *Good to Great*, HarperCollins, 2001.

Cross, Rob and Parker, Andrew. *The Hidden Powers of Social Networks*, HBS Press, 2004.

Csikszentmihalyi, Mihaly. *Flow – The Psychology of Optimal Experience*, Harper & Row, 1990.

Farmer, Neil and Lankester, Bob. *Total Business Design*, John Wiley & Sons, 1996.

Flood, Robert. *Rethinking the Fifth Discipline*, Routledge, 1999.

Fraser, George. *Click – Ten Truths for Building Extraordinary Relationships*, McGraw-Hill, 2008.

Gladwell, Malcolm. *The Tipping Point*, Little, Brown & Co, 2000.

Gobillot, Emmanuel. *The Connected Leader*, Kogan Page, 2007.

Gratton, Lynda. *Hot Spots*, FT Prentice Hall, 2007.

Grint, Keith. *Fuzzy Management*, Oxford University Press, 1997.

Hamel, Gary and Breen, Bill. *The Future of Management,* HBS Press, 2007.

Heskett, James L et al. *Putting the Service-Profit Chain to Work*, Harvard Business Review, March-April, 1994.

Hutton, Will. *The World We're In,* Abacus, 2003.

Kay, John. *Foundations of Corporate Success,* Oxford University Press, 1995.

Keller, Ed and Berry, John. *The Influentials,* Free Press, 2003.

Kennedy, Paul. *Preparing for the Twenty First Century,* HarperCollins, 1993.

Kohn, Alfie. *Punished by Rewards,* Houghton Mifflin, 1993.

Liker, Jeffrey. *The Toyota Way,* McGraw-Hill 2004.

Linley, Alex and Joseph, Stephen. *Positive Psychology in Practice,* John Wiley, 2004.

Nonaka, Ikujiro et al. *The Knowledge Creating Company,* Oxford University Press, 1995.

O'Shea, James and Madigan, Charles. *Dangerous Company,* Nicholas Brealey, 1997.

Pease, Alan and Barbara. *Why Men Listen & Women Can't Read Maps,* Orion Books, 2001.

Piercy, Nigel. *Market-led Strategic Change,*Butterworth-Heinemann, 2002.

Semler, Ricardo. *Maverick!,* Century, 1993.

Seddon, John. *I Want to Cheat,* Vanguard Education 1992.

Seddon, John. *The Case Against ISO 9000,* Oak Tree Press, 2000.

Seddon, John. *Freedom from Command and Control,* Vanguard Press, 2003.

Senge, Peter. *The Fifth Discipline,* Random House, 1993.

Snyder, CR and Lopez, Shane J. *Handbook of Positive Psychology*, Oxford University Press, 2002.

Stacey, Ralph. *Dynamic Strategic Management for the 1990s,* Kogan Page, 1990.

Surowiecki, James. *The Wisdom of Crowds,* Abacus, 2004.

The McKinsey Quarterly 2006, Number 3.

The McKinsey Quarterly 2007, Number 4.

The McKinsey Quarterly 2008, Number 1.

Von Krogh, Georg et al. *Enabling Knowledge Creation,* Oxford University Press, 2000.

Womack, James and Jones, Daniel. *Lean Thinking,* Simon & Schuster, 2003.

Index

The Innovative Management Programme

The *Innovative Management* Programme is a sponsored membership programme designed to help large and medium-sized private and public-sector organizations to innovate in their management practices to meet the challenges of a fast-changing world.

Neil Farmer, author of 'The Invisible Organization' and one of the UK's top independent change consultants has joined forces with Denis Bourne, founder of Magus Toolbox, probably the world's leading set of software products for social/organizational network analysis, to offer a step-by-step opportunity for your organization to investigate, test and then selectively embrace innovation in management – all at your own pace.

In recent years, more than 100 leading organizations in the USA have joined sponsored roundtable initiatives aimed at exploring the practical opportunities from social and organizational network analysis – learning how informal personal networks can be used to resolve many of the stubborn change and innovation problems that continue to frustrate managers today.

Although some of the most advanced work on innovative management has been carried out in the UK, particularly for business process outsource suppliers, awareness of these ideas has lagged behind in the UK and Europe. The *Innovative Management* Programme offers an opportunity for UK and European businesses to 'leapfrog' the American level of awareness. It also provides a window for leading-edge American and multi-national businesses to view their current knowledge and awareness of informal networks from a very different perspective.

The *Innovative Management* Programme allows sponsoring members to investigate, test and then selectively implement radical new management approaches at their own pace.

LEVEL 1 MEMBERSHIP – Investigation: from £7,500 + VAT

- An initial in-house 2-day *Innovative Management* workshop for between 5 and 20 people covering all aspects of practical innovative management and the software tools available – tailoring the resulting actions to meet your specific requirements.

- Quarterly research highlights plus question and answer service for 6 months.

LEVEL 2 MEMBERSHIP – Testing: 'Mix-and-match' fees from £25,000 + VAT

- Identification and ranking of key influencers at all levels in a sample population.

- Identification of hidden 'permissions' that drive local cultural behaviours.

- Mapping and workshop analysis of frequency/importance in selected informal employee communication networks that are necessary 'to get your jobs done efficiently'.

- Quarterly research highlights plus question and answer service for 12 months.

LEVEL 3 MEMBERSHIP – Implementation: Consultancy and software fees based on specific assignments

A 10 per cent discount on fees will apply to all current *Innovative Management Programme* members.

For more information, please contact Neil Farmer: neil.farmer@ informalnetworks.co.uk. Website: www.informalnetworks.co.uk.